ON

CHOMSKY

Morton Winston
The College of New Jersey

WADSWORTH

THOMSON LEARNING

Australia • Canada • Mexico • Singapore • Spain
United Kingdom • United States

Printed in the United States of America
2 3 4 5 6 7 04 03 02

For permission to use material from this text, contact us:
Web: http://www.thomsonrights.com
Fax: 1-800-730-2215
Phone: 1-800-730-2214

For more information, contact:
Wadsworth/Thomson Learning, Inc.
10 Davis Drive
Belmont, CA 94002-3098
USA
http://www.wadsworth.com

ISBN: 0-534-57640-0

TABLE OF CONTENTS

PREFACE

Noam Chomsky's seventieth birthday was the occasion for his many friends and admirers to send him birthday greetings and present him with papers written in his honor. While it is not unusual for influential scholars to be presented with a Festschrift upon attaining a venerable age, the style and content of this singular tribute to Noam Chomsky indicates how far-reaching and varied his influence has been. The essays represent disciplines of semantics, cognitive science, philosophy, phonology, morphology, psycholinguistics, computational linguistics, syntax, and politics. Blurbs on the backs of his book jackets regularly display a quote from the *New York Times Book Review* that describes him as "arguably the most important intellectual alive," but Chomsky, in his public lectures and interviews, likes to slyly remark that the jacket designers rarely go on to quote the following text that reads, "Since that's the case, how can he write such terrible things about American foreign policy?"[1]

During his career, now spanning more than forty-five years, Chomsky has attracted many devoted followers and admirers, as well as many critics and detractors. Because of the unconventional and often controversial nature of his views on many topics, it is often difficult for readers to gain an honest perspective on his thought. In addition to his prodigious output of published work – over seventy books and over a thousand articles – he has been the subject of documentary films, radio interviews, and has been active as a speaker and lecturer in North America, Europe, South America, and Australia. Over four thousand citations of his work are listed in the Arts and Humanities Citation Index, and he is one of the top ten most cited authors of all time.

In light of these challenges, my approach is that of brief intellectual biography rather than systematic analytical exposition. Chomsky is a living philosopher, and his thought is very much a work in progress. Consequently, I wanted to portray the *growth* of Chomsky's philosophy and to explain some of the links between the various concerns and ideas that animate it rather than present it as a finished whole. While I have tried to faithfully present Chomsky's views on major issues, I have had to use a rather broad brush. In order to avoid the over-simplified "Chomsky in 90 minutes" approach, I have attempted to place the development of his thought in some critical perspective and to provide interested readers with directions for further research. This book is a point-of-entry into Chomskyana; it is an invitation to explore more deeply Chomsky's own body of work and the even more voluminous secondary scholarship on him.

The research and writing of this short book was completed while I was on sabbatical leave from the College of New Jersey during the 1999-2000 academic year. I was privileged to spend several months during this period as a Fulbright Senior Scholar in the Program on Human Rights and Social Development of the Faculty of Graduate Studies, Mahidol University, Bangkok, Thailand. I gratefully acknowledge the support of the Committee for the Support of Scholarly Activity of the College of New Jersey, and I also wish to thank the Thailand-U.S. Educational Foundation, the Council for the International Exchange of Scholars, the U.S. Fulbright Committee, and the U.S. State Department for sponsoring my activities in Thailand. Special thanks are owed to Dr. Sriprapha Petcharamesree, director of the Human Rights and Social Development program at Mahidol, whose kindness made my stay in Thailand most enjoyable and productive, and to the students in my two graduate seminars who taught me much about the struggle for human rights in Southeast Asia.

I am particularly indebted to Noam Chomsky for granting me an interview. I have transcribed the tape of this interview, and portions of it are scattered throughout the text. The parts from the interview can be readily identified because they are left in interview format with M.W. as the questioner and N.C. as the respondent. The topics we discussed ranged widely over recent work in linguistics, the study of language acquisition related to the Minimalist Program, contemporary political issues, such as the protests in Washington over the World Bank and IMF, his views on the media, NATO's war in Kosovo, the Middle East, and several other matters. Quotations from Chomsky's major writings are cited in the text by means of abbreviations, a key to which can be found in the list of Chomsky's works at the end.

I would also like to thank several other individuals with whom I corresponded and discussed some of the ideas in this book, particularly: John Benditt, Julija Bogoeva, Dan Kolak, Gary Marcuse, and Nancy Nersessian.

M.W.
September 2000

1

DEVELOPMENT OF A DISSIDENT

The philosophers have only interpreted the world in various ways; the point, however, is to change it.

--Karl Marx "Theses on Feuerbach," XI (1845)

THE CONDITIONS OF GROWTH

Noam Chomsky is a linguist, philosopher, and social critic whose work has centered on the problems of human knowledge and human freedom. He belongs to the tradition of scholar-activists that includes Karl Marx, John Dewey, Albert Einstein, and Bertrand Russell. Chomsky has used his talents and energies not only to try to understand the bases of knowledge and creativity within human nature but also to transform contemporary social conditions in order to liberate the human creative potential. The pursuit of this humanistic ideal, both in his scholarship and in his political activism, has remained constant through Chomsky's career and provides a key to understanding the unity of his thought.

Chomsky's scholarly work in linguistics and related fields has focused on the problem of understanding the human capacity to learn a natural language. In his political writings, he has sought to reveal the characteristic forms of domination and oppression that characterize American global hegemony in the latter half of the twentieth century. It is sometimes difficult to see the connection between the two sides of his work. Chomsky himself has noted that one should not necessarily assume that there must be a strong connection between the two.[2] However, I believe there is. Chomsky himself addressed the same sort of question in his Russell Memorial Lectures given at Trinity College, Cambridge in 1971. After remarking that Russell, whose picture hangs on the wall inside Chomsky's office, was a philosopher who "sought not only to interpret the world but also to change it" Chomsky went on to ask, "Is there a common thread running through Russell's enormously varied studies, which, taken as a whole, touch on virtually every question of vital human concern? Is there, in particular, a link between his philosophical and political convictions?" [PKF x-xi]. In his second lecture, Chomsky found the missing link between Russell's empiricist epistemology and his politics in Russell's humanistic conception of man's intrinsic nature and his creative potential.

The link between the two sides of Chomsky's philosophy similarly lies in his own distinctive rationalist conception of human intelligence, which is quite different from Russell's empiricist view. Chomsky's rationalism emphasizes the specificity and biological rootedness of human knowledge while recognizing that our innate human cognitive capacities also provide the basis for the creative growth in our understanding of the world and of ourselves. In 1970 he wrote: "In investigating some of the most familiar achievements of human intelligence – the ordinary use of language, for example – we are struck at once by their creative character, by the character of free creation within a system of rules. Russell wrote that 'the humanistic conception regards the child as a gardener regards a young tree, i.e., as something with a certain intrinsic nature, which will develop into an admirable form, given proper soil and air and light" [PKF 50-51]. Following the implications of this gardening metaphor, Chomsky has in his scientific work tried to understand the intrinsic properties of the human mind that make creative cognitive growth possible. But while carrying on a vigorous scientific research program, he has also acted as a good gardener by opposing illegitimate systems of political and economic control that he views as depriving people of the proper conditions for human dignity and the realization of their human potentials. In Chomsky's own case, his family background, childhood, and college education were important influences on his intellectual development, and provide some clues as to how Noam Chomsky came to occupy the singular position of America's most famous dissident intellectual.

EARLY LIFE AND INFLUENCES

Noam Chomsky's father, Dr. William Chomsky, immigrated to America from his native Russia in 1913 and settled first in Baltimore, Maryland. He worked his way through Johns Hopkins University by teaching Hebrew. After marrying Elsie Simonofsky, Chomsky's mother, the couple moved to Philadelphia where both he and his wife taught Hebrew at the Mikveh Israel congregation.[3] Avram Noam Chomsky was their first child and was raised, along with his younger brother David, in a home that was filled with lively intellectual discussion. His parent's major goal in life was to contribute to the education of "individuals who are well-integrated, free and independent in their thinking, concerned about improving and enhancing the world, and eager to participate in making life more meaningful and worthwhile for all."[4] Judging from their eldest son's later accomplishments, they succeeded admirably.

Noam began his formal education just prior to the age of two when his parents enrolled him in the Oak Lane Country Day School, a university lab school run by Temple University that was heavily influenced by John Dewey's educational philosophy. According to Chomsky, his early education placed "a tremendous premium on individual creativity, not in the sense of slapping paints on paper, but doing the kind of work and thinking that you were interested in."[5] Noam was an avid reader from an early age, and devoured the classics of world literature such as Dickens, Dostoevsky, Tolstoy and others. He was also a regular student in his parents' Hebrew classes and was reading Hebrew literature at an early age. The circle of relatives and friends around the Chomsky household was made up largely of "normal Roosevelt Democrats," though he was also exposed to ardent Zionists, labor union organizers, pro-Bolshevik leftists, anti-Bolshevik socialists, and anarchists. Coming of age during the Great Depression, Noam has recounted how he remembers seeing "people coming to the door trying to sell rags and apples," and witnessing riot police beating up striking garment workers, events he now remembers as fostering the development of his political and social consciousness.[6]

Chomsky's first publication came shortly after his tenth birthday when he wrote an article for his school newspaper on the fall of Barcelona during the Spanish Civil War. He later described this event as "a big issue in my life at the time" that may well have been the origin of the libertarian and anarchist strands of his later political philosophy.[7] The Spanish uprising convinced him that there can be spontaneous, democratic expressions of the popular will, not controlled by any official ideology nor led by any party elite, that can rise up against systems of oppression. But the fall of Barcelona taught him that such spontaneous popular political movements are also liable to be brutally crushed by powers who like to settle arguments by force. Since the age of ten, Chomsky has been shocked and morally outraged by such brutal political repression, and has been "always on the side of the losers – the Spanish anarchists, for example."[8] During his teens, Chomsky was introduced to the thought of Rudolf Rocker, a Jewish anarchist, who wrote an influential book on the Spanish Civil War called *The Tragedy of Spain* and also to works by social-democratic Marxists, such as Karl Liebknecht, Rosa Luxemburg, and Karl Korsh.

The young Chomsky also read George Orwell's *Animal Farm*, a political allegory that struck him as "amusing but pretty obvious," as well as *Homage to Catalonia*, Orwell's account of the Spanish civil war. The latter impressed the young Chomsky greatly and confirmed his belief in the possibility of an anarchist or left-libertarian revolution succeeding were it not thwarted by fascist repression. Chomsky was certainly anti-fascist, but there is no evidence that he was ever attracted to Leninism or Stalinism, believing authoritarian dictatorship by the communist party to be another form of tyranny. On the other hand, neither was he ever much impressed by bourgeois democratic liberalism, even though the West did eventually enter the war against Nazi fascism, since, in the case of the United States, he understood that in state capitalist countries, society was dominated by the corporate class. The political ideas that Chomsky became sympathetic to at an early age were anarchism, left libertarian socialism, or radical democracy, all of which advocate forms of political organization in which the people govern themselves free from the domination of any ruling elites. According to his biographer, David Barsky, Chomsky "did not come to left-libertarian or anarchist thinking as a result of his disillusionment with liberal thought. He quite literally started there."[9]

After Oak Country Day School, Chomsky enrolled at Central High School in Philadelphia, an experience that convinced him that he was a good student, since for the first time he began to receive grades—good ones. But his high school experience was uncomfortable; he resented the emphasis on competition among students for grades, and what he felt was a system of indoctrination that blocked independent creative thinking. Eager for more intellectual stimulation, Chomsky began traveling to New York City on weekends where his uncle ran a newsstand on west Seventy-Second Street that functioned as a sort of informal salon for leftist Jewish intellectuals. On these weekends in New York, Chomsky learned about Freud, the internal machinations of Marxist politics, the working class labor movement in America, and no doubt much else. Another of Chomsky's role models at this time was Bertrand Russell, whose work in logic and the philosophy of language influenced his later thinking on linguistic grammar (see especially *The Logical Structure of Linguistic Theory*), and whose political activism encouraged Chomsky to believe that standing in solidarity with the oppressed, despite the personal and career sacrifices it might entail, was the correct choice for intellectuals with moral integrity. During his late teens, he was influenced by the literary critic Dwight MacDonald, who edited the leftist journal *Politics* from 1944-1949. Many years later Chomsky recalled how a piece by

MacDonald on the question of collective responsibility of the German and Japanese peoples for war crimes committed by their governments led him to question whether similar responsibility for the bombing of civilians, and the atomic destruction of Hiroshima and Nagasaki, should be laid at the feet of the American people: "to anyone whose political and moral consciousness had been formed by the horrors of the 1930s, by the war in Ethiopia, the Russian purge, the 'China incident,' the Spanish Civil War, the Nazi atrocities, the Western reaction to these events, in part, complicity with them—these questions had particular significance and poignancy."[10] Early on, Chomsky came to distrust the war propaganda that dominated the mainstream American media. He sought out alternative political perspectives from the left, and developed the habit of applying the same moral yardstick to all governments regardless of sympathy or ideology, judging them not by what they said, but by what they did.

EDUCATION AT THE UNIVERSITY OF PENNSYLVANIA

In 1945, at the age of sixteen, Chomsky began his undergraduate studies at the University of Pennsylvania. He lived at home and taught Hebrew classes on evenings and weekends to earn money to pay for his education. He began as a general liberal arts student but soon gravitated toward his philosophy instructor, C. West Churchman, and his instructor in Arabic, Giorgio Levi Della Vida. The latter, in particular, inspired him to believe in the possibility of Arab-Jewish cooperation on a libertarian socialist model in Palestine. Dissatisfied with the culture of academic elitism and competition at Penn, Chomsky toyed with the idea of dropping out of school and going to Palestine to join a kibbutz. But in 1947, two things persuaded him to stay in Philadelphia: he began dating a childhood friend, Carol Doris Shatz, whom he later married and who is still his wife, and he met the linguist Zellig Harris, the decisive intellectual influence on Chomsky's academic career.

Harris, who was an acquaintance of Chomsky's father, was by all accounts a charismatic figure. According to Chomsky he was, "a really extraordinary person who had a great influence on many young people in those days." Harris is mainly known for his work in structural linguistics and discourse analysis, but his interests ranged widely and included psychoanalysis and left-Zionist politics. Chomsky was drawn into Harris's circle in part because he found his open intellectual style congenial to his own. Harris' students regularly gathered off-campus for lively, far-ranging intellectual discussions, some of which lasted for days. Chomsky remembers these discussions as being "intellectually exciting as well as personally very meaningful experiences."

In 1947, Harris asked Chomsky to read the proofs of his *Methods of Structural Linguistics*. Chomsky later said he "found it very intriguing, and after some stimulating discussions with Harris, decided to major in linguistics as an undergraduate at the University of Pennsylvania."[11] Having studied historical linguistics and Medieval Hebrew grammar with his father, Chomsky decided to apply Harris' methods of structural analysis to that language. For his undergraduate thesis in 1949, he says he "tried to construct a system of rules for generating the phonetic forms of sentences, that is, what is now called a generative grammar. I thought it might be possible to devise a system of recursive rules to describe the form and structure of sentences, recasting the devices in Harris' *Methods* for this purpose, and thus perhaps to achieve the kind of explanatory force that I recalled from historical grammar."[12] A more developed version of this work, "The Morphophonemics of Modern Hebrew" became his Master's Thesis in linguistics in 1951 and was later published under that name.[13]

Here it is necessary to introduce some technical concepts from theoretical linguistics in order to understand what Chomsky was doing at this point in his career. During much of the nineteenth century, linguistics was understood mainly as a study of the historical or 'genetic' relationships among successive versions of the same natural language, e.g., English, Chinese, Russian, etc., and as an attempt to trace the history of the evolution of language-families, e.g., the Indo-European languages, the Romance languages, the Semitic languages etc., back to a single ancestral tongue. Languages that are now regarded as distinct, say English and German, have many resemblances, both on the level of form and on the level of meaning, for instance, the words *son* and *Sohn*, *mother* and *Mutter*, *seven* and *sieben*. This general historical approach to linguistics is termed 'diachronic' since it seeks to describe and explain the ways in which human languages change over historical time. The historical approach of the nineteenth century was in part a reaction against an earlier, speculative and philosophical approach to grammar of the Scholastics and their successors, the Port Royal grammarians of the seventeenth century, whose thought Chomsky was later to rediscover and resurrect to academic respectability. Nineteenth century historical linguistics was, like many of the then emerging fields of social science, strongly influenced by August Comte's positivism that stressed empirical methods of observation and analysis over philosophical speculation, and later, by Darwin, whose idea of evolution provided a fertile metaphor for understanding the development of many human social forms, including language. However, early in the twentieth century a radically new approach to the study of language emerged.

The Swiss linguist Ferdinand de Saussure is generally credited with being the founder of modern linguistics. In his *Cours de linguistique générale*, (a series of lecture notes collected by his students and published in 1915 after his death), he outlined the basic principles of the approach to the study of human language known as structuralism, that came to dominate the field during the first half of the century. Saussure argued that languages should be studied 'synchronically,' that is, at a single point in time, as systems of abstract formal relationships among structural elements. He also argued that the study of spoken language should be given priority over that of written language, and that grammar is a descriptive rather than a prescriptive inquiry. The goal of the linguist should be to construct a scientific theory of the structure of all human languages, one in which the observable data of languages are systematized and explained by means of a general theory of linguistic structure, not to evaluate people's speech according to some preferred prescriptive standard as correct or incorrect. It is sometimes claimed that Saussure's distinction between 'langue' and 'parole' (roughly between the language itself and speech) prefigures Chomsky's distinction between competence and performance, (roughly knowledge of the language versus use of that knowledge).[14] Whether or not that is accurate, Chomsky's own early approach to linguistics was thoroughly structuralist.

Following this general model, American structural linguists, such as Leonard Bloomfield, held that linguistic form can and should be studied independently of the meaning and use of language, that the methods of analysis used can be applied to all natural languages, and also that linguistics can be productively pursued as an autonomous science that need not borrow any of its basic explanatory principles from other fields of inquiry, such as psychology or sociology. Bloomfieldian linguistics was also methodologically 'behaviorist' in the sense that it insisted on the use of data that were directly observable and physically measurable, and in its rejection of 'mentalism', the belief in non-physical causes for behavior. Bloomfieldian linguistics regarded 'meaning' with suspicion and American linguistics charted a course in which it focused upon the formal properties of language as a system of elements and relations apart from its use as an instrument for communicating thoughts and ideas. The emphasis was on developing procedures that could be successfully used to determine what were the basic formal elements and relations that characterized the syntax and phonology of any given natural language independently of the meanings expressed.

The methods of structural linguistics that Chomsky learned from his mentor, Zellig Harris, were developed within this tradition. They were to be used by descriptive linguists "starting with the utterances which occur in a single language community at a single time, these procedures determine what may be regarded as identical in various parts of various utterances, and provide a method for identifying all the utterances as relatively few stated arrangements of relatively few stated elements."[15] But, as Harris realized, these methods and procedures of structural analysis, "do not eliminate non-uniqueness in linguistic descriptions," because it is possible for "different linguists, working on the same material, to set up different phonemic and morphemic elements, to break phonemes into simultaneous components or not to do so, to equate two sequences of morphemes as being mutually substitutable or not to do so."[16] The theoretical significance of the "non-uniqueness of linguistic descriptions" will become evident later on in relation to Chomsky's early attempts to develop an evaluation procedure for grammars.

In his undergraduate thesis, Chomsky attempted to construct a detailed grammar of Hebrew using Harris' methods. He found, not surprisingly, that there were many different ways of presenting the grammar, and began to wonder whether it might be possible to develop an idea of 'simplicity' for grammars that could be used to sort out the "linguistically significant generalizations" from among the alternative possible sets of grammatical rules. Later on, in *Syntactic Structures* (1957), he termed such a simplicity measure an 'evaluation procedure' and argued that it was not a reasonable goal for linguistic theory to attempt to gain a method more powerful than this for selecting among grammars, specifically ruling out the possibilities of there being a discovery procedure or a decision procedure for grammars. He puzzled about this question again when he was expanding his undergraduate thesis into his Master's Thesis in 1951. As he later recounted it, "My own work on Hebrew, though only rudimentary beyond the morphophonemic level, sufficed to suggest to me that something central was missing. The failure of inductive, data-processing procedures at the syntactic level became more obvious to me the more I worked on the problem" [LSLT 30].

THE SOCIETY OF FELLOWS AT HARVARD

After completing his Master's Thesis at Penn, Chomsky was given the opportunity to join the Society of Fellows at Harvard University, and in 1951 he moved to Cambridge, Massachusetts, where he has spent the rest of his career. It was an ideal environment for Chomsky, one in which he could give his creative intellect free rein. At Harvard and MIT, Chomsky encountered several individuals whose work turned out to have a decisive influence on the development of his thinking. He met Morris Halle, a fellow linguist and student of Roman Jakobsen, with whom he developed a close and lasting collegial relationship (they were the co-founders of the Department of Linguistics and Philosophy at MIT and still share an office there). He also met the logician Yehoshua Bar-Hillel, who had studied with Rudolf Carnap, and the information theorist Peter Elias, who was, like Chomsky, a Junior Fellow at Harvard. He also delved more deeply into philosophy and logic, particularly the work of the philosophers Nelson Goodman, who while at Penn had nominated Chomsky for the Society of Fellows, then moved to Boston himself at about the same time as his landmark work *The Structure of Appearance* was published in 1951, and Willard Van Orman Quine who was already at Harvard at the time giving lectures which resulted in landmark publications, such as his "Two Dogmas of Empiricism."[17] These influential analytic philosophers were developing their respective critiques of Logical Empiricism, and their work in logic and epistemology confirmed Chomsky's growing doubts about the adequacy of the methods of descriptive linguistics:

> Goodman's ongoing critique of induction seemed to point in a rather different direction, suggesting the inadequacy in principle of inductive approaches. Goodman's investigations of the simplicity of systems also suggested (to me at least) possibilities for a non-taxonomic approach to linguistic theory. Quine's critique of logical empiricism also gave some reason to believe that this line of inquiry might be a plausible one. Quine argued that the principles of scientific theory are confronted with experience as a systematic complex, with adjustment possible at various points, governed by such factors as general simplicity. Perhaps, then, analogous considerations hold for the fundamental problem of linguistic theory. [LSLT 33]

The 'fundamental problem of linguistic theory' that Chomsky refers to here was originally the linguist's methodological problem of selecting among competing descriptively adequate representations of the grammar of any particular natural language. It was a special case of the general problem of theory choice in science. But, following the 'Chomskyan Turn' he came to see this methodological problem in a different way, as analogous to the problem of determining how it is possible for children to acquire knowledge of a natural language. Chomsky came to see a parallelism between these two questions during the four years he spent as a Junior Fellow at Harvard working on the long manuscript of what was to become *The Logical Structure of Linguistic Theory*. As Chomsky notes, "In LSLT the "psychological analogue" to the methodological problem of constructing linguistic theory is not discussed, but it lay in the immediate background of my own thinking. To raise the issue seemed to me, at the time, too audacious" [LSLT 35]. No doubt under some pressure to finish his dissertation, Chomsky decided to defer the completion of the full text of LSLT, and to submit Chapter IX of it, "Transformational Analysis," which dealt with his innovative notions of linguistic levels and transformational rules, as his Ph.D. dissertation in linguistics at the University of Pennsylvania in 1955. That Fall, with the help of his friend, Morris Halle, he began teaching at MIT.

He is still there – as University Professor – forty-five years later. At first he worked in the Modern Languages Department and in the Research Laboratory of Electronics. During 1956-57 Chomsky revised the long manuscript of LSLT and submitted it to the MIT Press for publication, but it was rejected. He also prepared an article for a linguistics journal, which he says was rejected "virtually by return mail." There seemed to be little interest in what this unknown young linguist was thinking about. But that was soon to change.

2

THE CHOMSKYAN TURN IN LINGUISTICS

Colorless green ideas sleep furiously.

-- Noam Chomsky

THE ROUTE TO RATIONALISM

Nelson Goodman once remarked that he could "never follow the argument that starts from some interesting differences between parallel phrases such as 'eager to please' and 'easy to please' and that characterizes these differences as matters of 'deep' rather than 'surface' structure; and moves onto innate ideas."[18] My goal in this chapter is to explain how Chomsky first arrived at his hypothesis that human beings are equipped with an innate, species-specific language faculty that enables us to acquire the grammatical knowledge needed to speak and understand a first natural language, and then how this idea was developed into a more general 'Neo-Rationalist' epistemology and philosophy of mind and later into the P&P ('principles and parameters') approach that characterizes his most recent thinking on these issues. The general view I will defend is that the 'Chomskyan turn' in linguistics resulted from his creative synthesis of his novel approach to descriptive linguistics with insights about the nature of scientific theories that were characteristic of the Post-Positivist philosophy of science developing at that time. In particular, Chomsky was led to his 'innateness hypotheses' by means of a systematic analogy between the task that the linguist faces in constructing a descriptively adequate grammar of a natural language, and the task that the child faces in discovering the implicit rules of his or her language that define grammatical structure in that language.[19] In the first case, the linguist is attempting to construct a 'theory of a language' in the same sense as scientists who construct descriptive theories of other natural phenomena. However, following the Chomskyan turn, he came to view the second case, the childhood achievement in acquiring a first language, as a "psychological analogue" of the process by which linguists construct grammars, that is, as a process "akin to theory construction."[20] Chomsky's 1960 paper "Explanatory Models in Linguistics" was his first public discussion of this 'psychological interpretation' of grammar, but the ground for this shift had already been prepared in his first major publications in the late 1950s *Syntactic Structures*, and his influential review of B.F. Skinner's *Verbal Behavior.* [21] In order to follow the 'Chomskyan turn', it is first necessary that we understand his ground breaking work on the goals of linguistic theory developed in these earlier works.

SYNTACTIC STRUCTURES

In *Syntactic Structures*, Chomsky set out to show that any descriptively adequate grammar of a natural language, such as English, must contain at least three levels of description: the morphophonemic level that determines acceptable sound combinations and word constructions, the phrase structure level that determines acceptable constituent structure phrases, and a new level, the transformational level, that determines how grammatical sentences can be constructed from rearrangements of phrase structure elements. In *Syntactic Structures*, Chomsky appears to draw a boundary for linguistics at semantics, the study of word, phrase, and sentence meanings, arguing that meanings are not necessary in order to characterize the notion of "grammaticalness" – in his famous example:

(1) Colorless green ideas sleep furiously.

(2) Furiously sleep ideas green colorless.

Native speakers of English can recognize that the former is a grammatical but meaningless sentence, while the latter is neither grammatical nor meaningful. The exclusion of 'meanings' from the domain of linguistics was already part of the American descriptivist tradition. For Chomsky, the primary goal of linguistic analysis is to provide an account, or explanation, of the notion of 'grammatical sentence' in a particular language L. This explanation, Chomsky argues, must be capable of accounting not only for those sentences that have actually been produced or observed, but for "an indefinite number of new sentences" that would be recognized as grammatical by native speakers [SS 15]. That is, an ideal grammar of a natural language L can be seen as a device for 'generating' the infinite set of grammatical sentences of L. The emphasis on the 'creative' aspect of grammar was

16

not in keeping with Bloomfieldian tenets but had been discussed by other structural linguists such as de Saussure and Roman Jakobson. During our interview I queried him about the notion of linguistic 'creativity' he was attempting to account for in *Syntactic Structures*, as opposed to the more familiar idea of scientific, artistic, and cultural creativity:

N.C.: . . . this is a low level of creativity. It is what the seventeenth century thinkers called ordinary creativity, not extraordinary creativity. Nobody knows what our cognitive reach is, but there is every reason to believe that understanding extraordinary, genius level creativity is outside of our reach. There has been no progress on this question for 2000 years, literally none, not even a bad idea.

M.W.: So by 'creativity' here you mean only the creative aspect of grammars that allow speakers to recognize an infinite number of possible strings as grammatical in their languages?

N.C.: It is commonly said that the goal of a grammar is to understand how speakers recognize an infinite number of possible strings as grammatical. That's the way the question was opened just for motivation. It was immediately said that was not an issue. *Syntactic Structures* points out right away there is no reason to believe this category exists. Everybody misunderstands this. *Syntactic Structures* is mostly about what other people call semantics. I call it syntax. Semantics has to do with relating what's in the head to what's outside. Nobody talks about it. All the work that is called semantics is internal to the head, it is about symbol manipulation, and in a technical sense that's syntax, it's the area of syntax that probably has to do with language use. So we assume.

M.W.: So this is a strictly internalist approach.

N.C.: Yeah. And that includes formal semantics, possible world semantics, and everything else; it all works exactly the same way if it is a brain in a vat we are talking about. I mean look at the examples, "John is easy to please." "Flying planes can be dangerous." These are semantic issues in the sense that they have to do with the meaning of things, but they are all internalist semantics, which means they are syntax. The goal of the grammar is to provide the structure that underlies interpretation and use and articulation on the other side.

17

Assigning the right structure to "John is eager to please" and "John is easy to please." . . . One should not confuse it with true creativity, with artistic and scientific creativity, what Plato called a measure of madness.

These remarks clarify that from the start Chomsky was interested in orienting linguistics towards meaning, understood as relations between signs and mental concepts or interpretations, rather than as relations between words and things in the world. Chomsky's approach in *Syntactic Structures* to characterizing the ordinary ability of speakers to reliably and creatively assign the right syntactical structure, including an interpretation, to complex sentences was to apply formal, mathematical concepts derived from logic, finite automata theory, and recursive function theory, to the problem of constructing a descriptively adequate grammar of a natural language. In particular, he wanted to show how these formal methods supported the introduction of a new level of linguistic analysis – the transformational level. The general method he followed was to push "a precise but inadequate formulation to an unacceptable conclusion," in order to "expose the exact source of the inadequacy." [SS 5]. This method, incidentally, is Cartesian, and other applications of it can be found in his political thought.

Following this strategy, Chomsky first considered whether a grammar of English could be constructed using a *finite state language*, that is, one whose rules specified permissible transitions from one element to the next, left to right. He proved that finite state grammars could not in principle account for the fact that in English, for example, there are relationships among non-adjacent words, such as between the words *Anyone* and *lying* in the sentence *Anyone who says that candy bars are good for you is either lying or misinformed.*

He next analyzed a much more powerful approach to the construction of grammars, *phrase structure grammars*, which are usually illustrated by means of tree diagrams such as that in Figure 1 (page 19). Phrase structure rules were already used in linguistic analysis before Chomsky, but using his formalization, Chomsky was able to show that phrase structure grammars were, in principle, adequate to handle the data of English, but argued that "any grammar that can be constructed in terms of this theory will be extremely complex, *ad hoc*, and 'unrevealing', and that certain very simple ways of describing grammatical sentences cannot be accommodated...;" that is, grammars that rely wholly on phrase structure rules, while possible, would not be *simple* [SS 34].

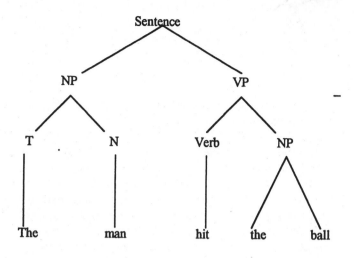

Figure 1 - Phrase Structure

The kinds of sentences that convinced Chomsky that this was the case, were, for instance, sentences like:

(3) The man hit the ball.

(4) The ball was hit by the man.

In (4), the passive voice is constructed from the active voice version in (3) by what Chomsky called a *transformational* rule that moves the noun in the verb phrase to the front of the sentence, moves the subject phrase to the back of the sentence, and substitutes *was hit by* for *hit*. Formally, a grammatical transformation T "operates on a given string (or set of strings) with a given constituent structure and converts it into a new string with a new derived constituent structure" [SS 44]. Chomsky had become convinced during his early work on Hebrew, and then later while he was working on LSLT, that such transformational rules were needed in order to capture "linguistically significant generalizations" that could not be accommodated by phrase structure grammars alone. He was thus led to postulate a third level of linguistic rules – transformations – in order to account for these kinds of data, and this hypothesis, in turn, led him to characterize the difference between the underlying phrase structure and new transformational structure as one of *deep* versus *surface structure*.

19

To see this distinction, let's go back to Goodman's complaint, the sentences:

(5) John is easy to please.

(6) John is eager to please.

On the surface these sentences may look like they have the same basic constituent structure. But then consider:

(7) It is easy to please John.

(8) It is eager to please John.*

Since it is possible to derive a grammatical sentence (7) by means of a transformation from (5), while it is not possible to derive (8) from (6), it follows that the two original sentences must have different deep structures. By multiplying examples of this kind, Chomsky was able to make a convincing case for accepting this new type of linguistic rule, transformations, and the associated notion of deep and surface levels of linguistic descriptions on the grounds that they would greatly simplify the presentation of the grammar.

But probably the most significant discussion in *Syntactic Structures* was in Chapter 6 "On the Goals of Linguistic Theory" in which he argued that the fundamental problem of linguistic theory was "the problem of justification of grammars" [SS 49]. As noted earlier, it was already accepted by Harris that the analytical methods of descriptive linguistics would not eliminate the problem of the non-uniqueness of grammars, that is, the fact that it is possible to present alternative, but incompatible, ways of delineating grammatical sentences in L. Chomsky had been thinking about this problem while working on LSLT, and he came to see it as a special case of the more general problem of theory choice in science that Goodman and Quine had been talking about. According to Quine, theory choice in science is *always* underdetermined by the evidence provided by empirical observations, so that it is not possible to account for why scientists accept their theories by means of the evidence provided by inductive methods alone – one always needs something else to constrain theory choice, for instance, some relevant notion of *simplicity*.[22] Goodman's critique of induction reinforced this argument by showing how the same observations could be interpreted as supporting the projection of different predicates – *green* in one case, and *grue* in the other – from observed to unobserved cases.[23]

Chomsky evidently accepted this general critique of Logical

20

Empiricism and came to believe that, "...choice of a best hypothesis in empirical science is not only underdetermined locally, that is, by particular samples from the data available in principle, but globally; that is, even given 'all data', there are variant hypotheses consistent with the data" [LSLT, p. 351]. This is why in *Syntactic Structures* he stressed the need to "clarify the criteria for selecting the correct grammar for each language" [SS 49], and he was led to consider the idea of a general *evaluation procedure* consisting of a rigorously defined notion of *simplicity* that would enable the linguist to evaluate different proposed grammars. He was careful to clearly distinguish the goal of developing a notion of 'linguistic simplicity' from the harder, and probably impossible, goals of developing a *discovery procedure* or a *decision procedure* for grammars, noting that, "There are few areas of science in which one would seriously consider the possibility of developing a general, practical, mechanical method for choosing among several theories, each compatible with the available data" [SS 53]. But, by setting his sights on even the modest goal of developing a rigorous notion of *linguistic simplicity*, Chomsky had already taken the first step towards rationalism and the innateness hypothesis.

CRITIQUE OF BEHAVIORISM

The second step was taken a few years later when he published a scathing review of an ambitious, but in Chomsky's view, deeply erroneous book by the leading American behaviorist psychologist, B. F. Skinner. In *Verbal Behavior*, Skinner attempted to extrapolate his theory of learning, based on the notions of stimulus, reinforcement, habit, conditioning, and response, that had been developed in order to explain relatively simple forms of animal learning, to the task of accounting for, and even controlling, a complex form of human behavior, the use of language. In his review, Chomsky argued that Skinner's attempt to extrapolate the explanatory concepts of behaviorist learning theory to human language robbed these terms of any determinate meaning, since "if we take his terms in their literal meaning, the description covers almost no aspect of verbal behavior, and if we take them metaphorically, the description offers no improvement over various traditional formulations."[24] His detailed refutations of the various elements of Skinner's theory, while individually impressive and convincing, are however, presented in light of a broader point that Chomsky urges at the beginning of this paper, namely, that it is highly implausible to suppose that the simple functional relationships between external events, stimuli and responses, presented by behaviorist learning theory can possibly explain complex behavior like human language learning. Skinner claimed to have shown that the contribution of the organism is not relevant or is of only minor importance, but Chomsky replied, "Careful study of this book (and of the research on which it draws) reveals, however, that these astonishing claims are far from justified." Rather, he suggested that, "One would naturally expect that prediction of the behavior of a complex organism (or machine) would require, in addition to information about external stimulation, knowledge of the internal structure of the organism, the ways in which it processes input information and organizes its behavior. These characteristics of the organism are in general a complicated product of inborn structure, the genetically determined course of maturation, and past experience." Already at this early stage, Chomsky was thinking about language learning as a task carried out by a kind of information-processing system with a particular complex in-built structure.

Consideration of Skinner's theory reinforced Chomsky's interest in the problem of language acquisition. What was left out of Skinner's theory was any remotely plausible account of linguistic knowledge, in particular, what Chomsky called syntax, that is, the part of the speaker's knowledge of the language that enables him to recognize the structures of an infinite number of sentences and to match up those structures with sound patterns and meanings, e.g., the knowledge of English that you are using to decode the strings of symbols that are presently streaming across your eyes that comprise this very long sentence. Chomsky, as we saw, had come to think about generative grammars as devices for generating the set of grammatical sentences of L, and as containing a notion of simplicity that would help decide what were linguistically significant generalizations. But now reflection on the problem of explaining language learning led him to conclude "the child who learns a language has in some sense constructed the grammar for himself on the basis of his observation of sentences and nonsentences (i.e., corrections by the verbal community). Study of the actual observed ability of a speaker to distinguish sentences from nonsentences, detect ambiguities, etc., apparently forces us to the conclusion that this grammar is of an extremely complex and abstract character, and that the young child has succeeded in carrying out what from the formal point of view, at least, seems to be a remarkable type of theory construction." This task, furthermore, "is accomplished in an astonishingly short time, to a large extent independently of intelligence, and in a comparable way by all children." These facts suggest, (but do not prove), that "human beings are somehow specially designed to do this, with a data-handling or 'hypothesis-formulating' ability of unknown character and complexity." Thus the two problems, the methodological problem of constraining theory choice in linguistics, and the problem of explaining language learning, began to converge. They eventually merged as Chomsky worked out the theoretical implications of the 'psychological analogue' to his theory of grammar.

THE STANDARD THEORY

To follow the 'Chomskyan turn' one must appreciate the systematic ambiguity with which Chomsky intends the statement: *A grammar of L is essentially a theory of L.* On the literal reading, the terms *grammar* and *theory* refer to the systems of explicit formal rules that professional linguists use to describe the structure of languages. But, from about 1960 onward to about 1980, comprising what has been called Chomsky's "classic period" or "The Standard Theory," Chomsky uses these terms to also refer to the speaker's *internalized knowledge of language* or his linguistic *competence*. Competence, or knowledge of grammar, is not the same as language use, or *performance*, any more than knowing a scientific theory, for instance, organic chemistry, is the same as using that knowledge to derive predictions in specific cases or to make useful compounds. Linguistic competence is an idealized notion that is abstracted from actual speech in that it is regarded as "unaffected by such grammatically irrelevant conditions as memory limitations, distractions, shifts of attention and interest and errors (random or characteristic) in applying the knowledge of the language in actual performance" [ATS 3]. A theory of the speaker's linguistic competence then is only one part of a complete theory of language use, but it is a crucial part, because it addresses the fundamental fact about linguistic behavior that "the speaker, on the basis of a finite and somewhat accidental experience with language, can produce utterances which are new both to him and to other speakers, but which are immediately recognizable as utterances belonging to the language" [LSLT 113]. This ability is captured in transformational generative grammars by the use of recursive rules, such as the one that allows us to reiterate adjectives like *very* in statements like, *This is potentially a very, very, very, very, very, ... etc., long sentence.*

This creative aspect of language make it extremely implausible to suppose that in learning a language what one has done is merely absorb a set of sentences to which he has been exposed. Rather, the language learner "has also abstracted from this set of sentences, somehow, and learned a certain structural pattern to which these sentences conform, and he can add new elements to his linguistic stock by constructing

23

new sentences conforming to this structural pattern." Linguistic *competence*, like a theory, enables one to "go beyond" what has been observed. Competence is the 'tacit theory' of the language that speakers have somehow learned, which Chomsky also refers to as the "grammar of L" when using this term in its psychological sense.

We saw earlier that Chomsky's view of theories was influenced by Goodman's and Quine's critiques of Logical Empiricism. In particular, Chomsky accepted the view that choice among scientific theories is *always* underdetermined by experience. This general fact about theories is also known as the "poverty of the stimulus argument." It is, on Chomsky's rationalist view of knowledge, impossible to account for the fact that people are able to develop the sorts of rich and complex systems of ordinary knowledge they come to possess, such as their linguistic competence, on the assumption that they somehow induce them from the limited and partial evidence of experience. In order to solve this problem, what James McGilvray calls "Plato Problem" (after the famous story of the slave boy who 'knew" geometry from the *Meno)*, Chomsky was led to the hypothesis that children come equipped with something that functions like an innate theory of language that determines the basic structure of all human languages. It is likely that he also accepted several other ideas about theories: for instance, the idea that observation is somehow "theory-dependent," in that one needs to have some kind of prior theory or hypothesis about what one is looking for in order to see it; and the idea that there is no "logic of discovery" that enables scientists to get to the truth of things by means of a mechanical procedure. There are also a number of other commonsense ideas about the nature of theories that might be relevant as background for his thinking at the time, for instance, the idea that theories are about specific types of things or events, e.g., the cause of AIDS, not about "things in general;" that they sometimes cause us to see things in different ways, e.g. "Sun rises" becomes "Earth turns;" that they are comprised of hypotheses that go beyond direct observations, e.g.; "The universe is filled with dark matter;" and that theories are sometimes tacit or unconscious, e.g., *"You can't lose something you never had."* (probably something you believe but never stated in so many words).

In saying that *A grammar of L is essentially a theory of* L, Chomsky was suggesting an analogy between the linguist's task of constructing a grammar, and the child's task of learning a first language; both were conceived as tasks of 'theory construction.' But how good is this analogy really? While the linguist must follow an arduous and drawn out process of 'conjecture and refutation' in learning what constitutes a significant generalization about the

24

language he or she is studying. But the child masters the grammar of the first language to which he or she is exposed with little or no explicit instruction in a remarkably brief time. The analogy seems to break down because children do succeed in acquiring a grammar of L (in the psychological sense), while the linguist may or may not succeed in constructing a grammar of L (in the scientific sense). But, rather than discrediting the analogy, from Chomsky's vantage point this difference became the prime motivation for the 'innateness hypothesis':[25]

> It seems plain that language acquisition is based upon the child's discovery of what from a formal point of view is a deep and abstract theory—a generative grammar of his language—many of the concepts and principles of which are only remotely related to experience by long and intricate chains of unconscious quasi-inferential steps. A consideration of the character of the grammar that is acquired, the degenerate quality and narrowly limited extent of the available data, the striking uniformity or the resulting grammars, and their independence of intelligence, motivation, and emotional state, over wide ranges of variation, leaves little hope that much of the structure of the language can be learned by an organism initially uninformed as to its general character. [ATS 58]

In other words, in order to account for first language acquisition, on the assumption that what is learned is a kind of 'theory', it becomes plausible to hypothesize that children have an innate, species-specific, *language acquisition device* [LAD] of some kind that is employed somehow when they learn the 'grammar of L.' The LAD functions for the child as a *discovery* procedure would function for the linguist (if such a thing were possible), since it provides a reliable method for actually arriving at the 'grammar of L' on the basis of exposure to a corpus of utterances of L. The linguist has no initial idea about what this device consists of but can reasonably believe that it works equally well for all natural languages since it enables children to successfully learn the grammar of whatever natural language he or she is exposed to in early childhood. It is highly unlikely that there is much variation within the human species as to the structure of this special innate endowment, since, for instance, a child of Japanese ancestry raised in London will learn English, while a child of English ancestry raised in Japan will learn to speak Japanese. In order to account for these elementary facts, it seems reasonable to suppose that the LAD contains a cognitive blueprint of some kind for all human languages.[26]

Following the implications of this line of reasoning, Chomsky was led to think of the task of developing a criterion of linguistic simplicity for selecting among proposed linguistic grammars as the search for the principles of a *universal grammar*. Within the Standard Theory (dating from *Aspects of the Theory of Syntax* onward), the goal of developing an evaluation measure is redefined as the goal of discovering *linguistic universals*, that is, "general assumptions about the nature of language...from which particular features of the grammars of individuals languages can be deduced" [ATS 46]. A *universal grammar* [UG] is a "system of principles, conditions, and rules that are elements or properties of all human languages, not merely by accident, but by necessity—of course, I mean biological, not logical necessity" [RL 29]. Because a UG expresses "the essence of human language" it can also serve as a description of what "language learning must achieve," and thus will provide a clue to the constitution of the LAD. In particular, if we can make the simplifying assumption that language learning takes place instantaneously, then an 'innateness hypothesis' concerning the constitution of the human language acquisition device will consist of "principles for the preliminary, pre-theoretic analysis of data as experience...; properties of the UG which determine the character of what is learned....and possibly other principles" [RL 34]. Thus Chomsky came to hypothesize that the child's initial observation of a language must depend upon some prior innate 'theory of language,' and also that the principles of the UG can be construed as an innate property of the human mind.

But, he emphasizes that such a highly idealized hypothesis is only a starting point for further research, since it could obviously turn out that the assumption that language learning is instantaneous may have to be revised, and this would force us to modify the assumption that certain properties of the UG are present in the initial state. It might also turn out that the LAD can only operate with the assistance of other faculties of mind, such as those that construct our 'commonsense understanding' of the natural and social worlds. There are in fact many ways to falsify the initial research hypothesis. It is just that they all require specific kinds of empirical evidence. Here then is another instance in which Chomsky's scientific methodology consists in pushing a precise but inadequate formulation to an unacceptable conclusion. He in effect laid down a challenge to the scientific community to prove him wrong or prove him right. It was a challenge that many researchers accepted, thereby launching a scientific revolution in linguistics and related fields.[27]

In this respect, Chomsky's major contribution to linguistics and related fields of study can be seen as one in which he laid out a *research programme* under which the study of language and mind could conceivably progress towards deep and important insights about the specific nature of the human cognitive capacity. Most of twentieth century social science was conducted under the influence of Logical Empiricism in philosophy, Behaviorism in psychology, and Descriptivism in linguistics, views that all held that the study of the human mind was neither possible nor scientifically respectable. Chomsky's proposals for a 'science of mind,' using the study of grammar as a point of entry, struck many researchers as a new option, and as an intellectual challenge.

It is sometimes claimed that Chomsky's work in the 1960s created a 'scientific revolution' in linguistics and psychology, but Chomsky himself, with characteristic modesty, is circumspect about endorsing such claims.[28] In fact, rather than claiming that his ideas about universal grammar and innateness were novel or revolutionary, he instead went back into the history of philosophy and linguistics in order to argue that his views were in fact best seen as a revival of ideas that had been around for several centuries, but had been largely forgotten by twentieth century philosophy and science.

CARTESIAN LINGUISTICS

Chomsky's 'revolutionary' theory of grammar drove a stake into the heart of the dominant empiricist paradigm of the 1950s. For most researchers during this period, there seemed "little reason to question the conviction of Leonard Bloomfield, Bertrand Russell, and positivistic linguists, psychologists, and philosophers in general that the framework of stimulus-response psychology would soon be extended to the point where it would provide a satisfying explanation for the most mysterious human abilities" [LM2]. The development of the computer and of information theory also encouraged many to believe that 'machine translation' of human speech was right around the corner. But by the end of the decade, the confidence in this empiricist approach to the study of human knowledge began to dissolve, and Chomsky deserves no small portion of the credit for showing why it was inadequate. But, according to Chomsky, "It makes sense, I think, to view what happened in the 1950s as a confluence between ideas that have a traditional flavor but that had been long forgotten, and a new understanding that made it possible to approach at least some of the traditional questions in a more serious ways than heretofore" [PP 8].

Chomsky notes that, "I didn't begin writing about intellectual history until the early 1960s."[29] Once he got started, however, Chomsky found historical antecedents of his own approach in the philosophy of Plato (470-342 BC), who believed that knowledge was recollection; in the great seventeenth century mathematician and philosopher René Descartes (1596-1650); in the works of Cartesians such as the Port-Royal grammarians; and in the thought of the nineteenth century linguist Wilhelm von Humboldt (1767-1835) and the American pragmatist Charles Sanders Peirce (1839-1914). Chomsky's interest in tracing the historical lineage of his brand of rationalism began in earnest in 1964, while he was a fellow of the American Council of Learned Societies, and in lectures he gave that year at Princeton. His study of the history of rationalist ideas about human language and human knowledge ideas was later published in *Cartesian Linguistics: A Chapter in the History of Rationalist Thought* (1966), and elements of this historical research appear subsequently in many of his writings.

Chomsky was attracted to Descartes in part because of the latter's interest in the phenomenon of human creativity. Descartes had argued that human mental activities, particularly in the use of language and in the exercise of the will could not possibly be explained or predicted by means of mechanical laws. Chomsky refers to Descartes' discovery of the limits of physical explanation as the 'first cognitive revolution'. Descartes wrote, for instance, "It is a very remarkable fact that there are none so depraved and stupid, without even excepting idiots, that they cannot arrange different words together, forming of them a statement by which they make known their thoughts; while, on the other hand, there is no animal, however, perfect and fortunately circumstanced it may be, which can do the same" [CL 116-117]. For Descartes, non-human animals were mere 'automata,' whose behavior could in principle be accounted for as one accounts for the behavior of machines, and indeed of all physical objects, by means of physical laws that assumed that all forces were communicated by contact. However, Descartes argued that the human abilities to 'think,' to 'decide,' and to use language creatively could not be accounted for in this way. The explanation of these distinctively human abilities, for Descartes, required belief in 'innate ideas' that were lodged in an immaterial 'soul' or *res cogitans,* a 'thinking thing' that was conceived by him and his followers to be utterly distinct from the physical body.

Chomsky does not, of course, follow Descartes in accepting metaphysical dualism, believing instead that the 'innate ideas' that make human language possible reside in our biological constitution,

28

wired somehow into our brains. But, he does believe that Cartesian psychology, even "with all its gaps and deficiencies, is an argument that must be taken seriously" [LM 7]. It is a serious argument because it points to the fact that certain properties of human cognition, such as creativity, freedom from stimulus control, and its complexity cannot be explained by means of 'empiricist' learning principles. Agreeing with Descartes, Chomsky holds that the "creative aspect of normal language use is one fundamental factor that distinguishes human language from any known system of animal communication" [LM 100].

However, there is another, less remarked-upon aspect of Chomsky's 'Cartesianism;' that is, his use of formal, mathematical techniques and idealizing assumptions that are reminiscent of those that Descartes discussed in his famous works on scientific method: *Discourse on Method* (1637) and *Rules for the Direction of the Mind* (1628). Descartes believed the human mind was equipped (by God) with a 'natural light of reason' by use of which human beings could attain reliable knowledge of the natural world. However, we have to learn how to use this innate faculty, sometimes called 'Cartesian common sense,' correctly, which requires following certain rules of method. Among the most important rules that Descartes recommended were that in researching any complex question one begins by dividing it up into simpler parts, solving the simplest problems first and only then moving to the more complex and difficult ones; that one should provide precise definitions of key theoretical terms; and that one should attempt to apply formal mathematical methods wherever possible. In his later theorizing on the human-science forming capacity, Chomsky suggests that there is an intuitive notion of 'simplicity' or 'conceptual naturalness' that guides scientific theory construction and which includes principles such as economy, symmetry, and non-redundancy— an updated relative of Cartesian common sense.[30]

Following this methodological advice, Chomsky has consistently argued that the scientific study of language and of mind may be able to progress under certain 'abstractions' or idealizing assumptions, such as that competence can be considered as distinct from performance, that syntax (in the broad internalist sense) can be usefully studied apart from semantics (i.e., how language relates to the world), that language learning can be assumed to be instantaneous, and so forth. These are for Chomsky, 'working hypotheses,' that are justified only "by the success that is achieved when [they] are adopted" [LM 111]. He thinks that these idealizing assumptions are for the time being justified because "many quite elegant results have been achieved on the basis of these abstraction[s]." Yet, he is quite willing to admit, that they may

eventually have to be abandoned if the study of language and mind is to advance further [LM 112]. This method of pushing a precise but inadequate theory to its limits in order to discover the reasons why it fails, is a staple of Chomsky's approach to science, and helps to explain why linguistics has undergone a series of what philosophers of science call 'progressive problem shifts' from the Standard Theory of the 60s and 70s to the Principles and Parameters (P&P) approach of the 1980s and then on to the Minimalist Program of 90s.

M.W.: Your work is very Cartesian, isn't it? I mean specifically your methodological approach to science.

N.C.: All of this is Cartesian. Not only the methods. There are even specific Cartesian conclusions. Look at the Cartesian conception about the way the mind is organized. Sure his physics collapsed pretty quickly, but the psychology and what became neurophysiology, that remains, and it looks pretty accurate.

M.W.: But I was referring to Cartesian methods, his rules for the direction of the mind, you know, divide a complex problem into its simplest parts, address the easiest questions first, use formal mathematical models wherever you can, and so forth, as opposed to, say, trying to reduce everything to physics.

N.C.: That's just science. Reductionism is not part of science. If you look at the history of science occasionally you get reduction, but not very much. Take chemistry and physics. Until the 1930s chemistry couldn't be related to physics, and it was never reduced to classical physics. What happened is that physics had to undergo a radical revolution--the quantum theoretical revolution—before it could be united with an unchanged chemistry. The same could well happen in the study of mind.

M.W.: But it's very premature, isn't it, to suppose we are close to being able to reduce psychology to neuroscience?

N.C.: It is not only premature; it is silly. If you look at the hard sciences, it doesn't work that way. In case after case the fundamental science had to be radically modified in order for it to be unified with the unchanged higher-level science.

M.W.: So if you translate this experience to neuroscience and cognitive psychology, do you think then we are going to have to have a radical transformation of our understanding of the brain before we can even think about reducing psychology?

N.C.: Look, in the 1920s you could not have predicted how chemistry and physics would ever be related, if indeed they would be. And those are fields that are way better understood than these. And if you go back a couple of centuries earlier the same is true. You couldn't tell whether electromagnetic theory could be reduced to mechanics. It turned out it was, but you couldn't know. In these cases virtually nothing is known about the brain. We can speculate now, but there is not much point.

The history of science is littered with discarded theories, and studying them can provide a reality check on just how difficult real progress in human understanding is. Chomsky's own historical research into the history of linguistics identified the Port-Royal Grammar of 1660 as an early attempt to develop the study of language along Cartesian lines. The grammarians of Port-Royal were interested in developing a 'philosophical grammar' that would reveal the common underlying principles of the organization of expressions in vernacular languages such as French and in this respect represented a break with the Scholastic tradition which had focused almost exclusively on Latin. Chomsky credits these scholars with having recognized the importance of phrases as key elements in grammatical structure, and with having anticipated, to some extent, his own distinction between 'deep' and 'surface' structure, in the way that they distinguished between the physical aspect of speech, the sound pattern, and the underlying meanings or propositions that speech conveyed.

He also studied the work the German linguist Willem von Humbolt who, like the Cartesians, laid stress on the creative aspect of language use, and who in the early nineteenth century puzzled over how it is possible for languages to make 'infinite use out of finite means'. But while von Humbolt correctly identified accounting for creativity as the key problem of linguistic theory, he really didn't have a theory that might account for it. But, according to Chomsky:

N.C.: . . . that's true of human affairs generally. There are no theories. It's just too hard. Theories can be developed in very narrow areas. Even in physics, by the time you get to even minimal complexity, it's out of sight. That's why linguistics works. It works in very specific areas. So take the creativity issue. Go back to that. Take the Humboldian idea that we are studying the infinite use of finite means. But we're not studying that. We are studying the means. We are not studying the use. To study the use of finite means is out of sight. Way too hard. There are no theories about use. The same is true of, say, robotics or how you organize motion. Like how do I reach for a cup? It turns out to be a very hard problem. The signal goes to my elbow, there is a positional program of some kind; it's very tricky. There are some interesting ideas about it, mostly for cockroaches. But if you ask why is the cockroach turning left, you don't know. You don't even ask that kind of question. There is no framework in which to even raise the question. It's just not the kind of problem we know how to deal with.

Chomsky's historical research also turned up a little known paper by the American pragmatist, Charles Sanders Peirce entitled "The Logic of Abduction" in which he argued that the history of science demonstrates that there must be some kind of innate 'guessing instinct' that enables human beings to correctly guess the laws of nature: "Man's mind has a natural adaptation to imagining correct theories of some kinds....If man had not the gift of a mind adapted to his requirements, he could not have acquired any knowledge" [LM 91]. Peirce termed this faculty of reasoning to the best hypothesis 'abduction', and he distinguished it from mere 'induction', which he said, "has no originality in it but only tests a suggestion already made." Seizing on this idea, Chomsky speculates that it may be possible to develop a "Peircean logic of abduction" that will describe the innate capacities that comprise human intelligence, as well as its innate limits. This line of thought led him in the 1970s to propose a general research program for developing cognitive psychology as a genuine science of the mind.

LANGUAGE AND MIND

As the Standard Theory was developed, it gradually became clear that Chomsky's approach to the study of language could be seen as a model for a more general approach to doing psychology. This assumption is evident already in *Language and Mind* (1966) in which Chomsky claims that, "'...the study of language should occupy a central place in general psychology" [LM 99], and in his other writings from this period, for instance, when he opined that:

Both a grammar of a particular language and a general theory of language are of interest primarily because of the insight they provide concerning the nature of mental processes, the mechanisms of perception and production, and the mechanism by which knowledge is acquired....It seems quite obvious that it is within this general framework that linguistic research finds its intellectual justification.[31]

But the view is most clearly expressed in the first chapter of *Reflections on Language* in which he attempts to explain how, by studying the properties of natural languages, "we may hope to gain some understanding of the specific characteristics of human intelligence:"

One reason for studying language—and for me personally the most compelling reason—is that it is tempting to regard language, in the traditional phrase, as 'a mirror of mind.' I do not mean by this simply that the concepts expressed and distinctions developed in normal language use give us insight into the patterns of thought and the world of 'common sense' constructed by the human mind. More intriguing, to me at least, is the possibility that by studying language we may discover abstract principles that are universal by biological necessity and not mere historical accident, that derive from the mental characteristics of the species. [RL 4]

He quotes Bertrand Russell from his classic 1948 work *Human Knowledge: Its Scope and Limits,* who wondered, "How comes it that human beings, whose contacts with the world are brief, personal, and limited, are nevertheless able to know as much as they do know?" and proceeds to reject both the skeptical and the empiricist answers to prepare the way for a discussion of his own biological-rationalist approach. The skeptics answer the question by denying that we humans do in fact have any significant knowledge, while empiricists argue that we acquire our knowledge by induction from sensory experience. But for Chomsky, the answer to Russell's query lies in the fact that,

...our systems of belief are those the mind, as a biological structure, is designed to construct. We interpret experience as we do because of our special mental design. We attain knowledge when the 'inward ideas of the mind itself' and the structures it creates conform to the nature of things. [RL 7-8]

33

Presumably this pre-established harmony between the human mind and Nature is the result of the millions of years of biological evolution during which the human species evolved. But according to Chomsky, evolutionary explanations are premature and somewhat beside the point, since we can only speculate about our distant evolutionary past. On the other hand, we have the finished product, the human mind/brain readily at hand, so "Why then, should we not study the acquisition of a cognitive structure such as language more or less as we study some complex bodily organ?" [RL 10], that is, as it unfolds during maturation from infancy to adulthood. He notes that it is a "curious fact about the intellectual history of the past few centuries that physical and mental development have been approached in quite different ways" [RL 9]. In the early part of the 20th century, the dominant idea in psychology was that there would be some 'general learning theory' common to both humans and other species that would explain how we come to possess the kinds of knowledge we have. While in biology, "it is taken for granted that the physical structure of the organism is genetically determined, though of course variation along such dimensions as size, rate of development, and so forth will depend in part upon external factors" [RL 9]. Why not assume the same about cognitive development? The notion of a general learning theory has "proved rather barren" and the "position has little to recommend it on grounds of empirical evidence or inherent plausibility or explanatory power," and now "serves as an impediment, an insurmountable barrier to fruitful inquiry, much as the religious dogmas of an earlier period stood in the way of the natural sciences" [RL 12].

Chomsky now largely abandons his earlier talk about language acquisition being akin to a process of theory construction, and shifts to using an overtly biological metaphor, that of the growth of bodily organs, as a way of talking about the phenomenon of language and human knowledge more generally. This biological metaphor is characteristic of his later classic period, sometimes called the Extended Standard Theory (ETS), before he shifted again to the 'Principles and Parameters' (P&P) approach of his most recent work. In his presentation of the EST in *Reflections on Language* (1975), he asks us to consider how a 'neutral scientist' might proceed to develop a 'learning theory' for a particular sort of cognitive attainment.

> The natural first step would be to select an organism, O, and a reasonably well delimited cognitive domain, D, and to attempt to construct a theory that we might call 'the learning theory for the organism O in the domain D.' This theory—call it LT(O,D)—can be regarded as a system of principles, a

34

mechanism, a function, which has a certain 'input' and a certain 'output' (its domain and range respectively). The 'input' to the system LT(O,D) will be an analysis of the data in D by O; the 'output' (which is, of course, internally represented, not overt and exhibited) will be a cognitive structure of some sort. This cognitive structure is one element of the cognitive state attained by O. [RL 14]

Proceeding then in a systematic and rational manner our neutral scientist should then pass through the following stages of inquiry:

Set the cognitive domain D.

Determine how O characterizes data in D 'pre-theoretically,' thus constructing what we may call 'the experience of O in D'.

Determine the nature of the cognitive structure attained: that is, determine as well as possible, what is learned by O in the domain D.

Determine LT (O,D), the system that relates experience to what is learned. [RL 15]

The D chosen should be reasonably well delimited so as to make the task manageable; we should not skip over steps 2 and 3, since "it is senseless to try to relate two systems—in this case, experience and what is learned—without some fairly good idea of what they are" [RL 16]. Only after having developed LT(O,D)s for a variety of organisms in a variety of specific cognitive domains are we in a position to meaningfully ask the more general question: "What is a learning theory? Or better: "Is there such a theory as learning theory?" [RL 17]. Specifically, we can ask two questions:

Is it the case that however we select O and D, we find the same LT(O,D)?

Are there significant features common to all LT(O,D)'s?

Surely, Chomsky argues, even given the little that we presently know, the answer to the first question must be "a firm No," since if we take O to be humans (H) and and O' rats I, D to be language (L) and D' to be maze running (M), hypothesis 1 would imply that humans would be "as much superior to rats in maze-learning ability as they are in language-learning ability. But this is so grossly false that the question cannot be seriously entertained." Question 2 is at least a 'starter,' but the problem here is that the question is "hopelessly premature." We simply have not done the work necessary, in detail, for significant Os and Ds to be at present in a position to answer it. Thus, he concludes, "for the present, there seems to be no reason to suppose that learning theory exists" [RL 19-20]. Despite his skepticism, what emerges from this discussion is the conception of a scientific research program for cognitive science, one which systematically explores the nature of the human cognitive capacity by characterizing the product, what is learned, the input, the organism's experience, and by developing quite specific and detailed LT's that relate the one with the other. Within this general framework, we can pose a third type of question:

> Whether there is some interesting set of domains $D_1 \ldots D_n$ such that $LT(O, D_1) = LT(O, D_j)$; or $LT(O, D_i)$ is similar in interesting ways to $LT(O, D_j)$. [RL 20]

Chomsky again expresses skepticism that there is known to be any such similar domains of learning in humans, but he admits "the possibility is not excluded". We can try to discover specific domains of human cognitive capacity that might be similar in important respects to human language learning, but there is in his view "no particular reason to expect there is such a domain". What we can do, however, is to develop cognitive science along the lines indicated and study in various domains the innate capacities of humans (and other psychological organisms) "to construct cognitive structures, that is, to learn" [RL 22].

This general methodological framework has been called the 'modular approach,' and has guided much of what goes by the name of 'cognitive science' for the past twenty-five years.[32] It holds that in studying such a complex phenomenon as human knowledge it is best to divide the mind into more or less independent 'faculties' or 'modules' and to study their structures in detail before one attempts to determine how they interact with other cognitive systems. So, for example, it makes methodological sense to try to study syntax separately from phonology, on the one hand, and language use on the other, since there is reason to believe that the grammar is a 'module' having its own quite specific properties. Similarly for face recognition, episodic memory, musical memory, and other specific cognitive capacities. By systematically building up our understanding of the precise properties of specific cognitive modules, and only then attempting to see how they might be functionally related within the cognitive system as a whole, we can hope to make progress in understanding and perhaps explaining how as complex an organ as the human mind/brain actually works.

But progress in such an endeavor is by no means guaranteed. It could be, he goes on to speculate, that understanding how the human mind works is beyond the 'human science-forming capacity.' There must, he thinks, also be LT(H,D)'s that provide for "the vast and impressive scope of scientific understanding" and which also "sharply constrain the class of humanly accessible sciences" [RL 25]. The general idea that there are limits to human understanding is ancient and not at all implausible – dogs and cats are incapable of learning algebra – so why should we assume that we are not incapable of learning certain things? In fact, "thinking of humans as biological organisms in the natural world, it is only a lucky accident if their cognitive capacity happens to be well matched to scientific truth in some area" [RL 25]. For topics that lie outside the human science-forming capacity, the answers to questions we ask "will always be shrouded in mystery." The question about the limits of human knowledge, particularly knowledge about the biological roots of human social and political behavior was one of the questions I put to Chomsky in our interview:

M.W.: How do you reconcile your commitment to strong innate determinants for human language and perception with your skepticism about the viability of parallel hypotheses in the domains of human economic, social and political behavior?

N.C.: I just take for granted that everything we do, in our moral judgments, our behavior, our social systems, and so forth, mainly flows out of our innate nature. There is no possible way to acquire a culture otherwise. So what's the skepticism? It's about what people say about it. What people say about it is, well, for instance, you'd like to believe that society ought to be authoritarian so you say that people are authoritarian. It's the same with the [Steven] Pinker and [E.O.] Wilson stuff. You can't do anything with reverse engineering. You can't even work out the reverse engineering of a machine. Take a look at humans. Take the few things that are known about language. The structure of the ear happens to be extremely well adapted to language; you have all these bones in just the right place. So you do reverse engineering. Trouble is it started 160 million years ago with mice when the reptilian jaw split. That's why biologists laugh at this stuff. You can't do it.

M.W.: So you think you can't study the biological bases of human culture in a scientific way, only just as speculation?

N.C.: It's not even speculative science, its just literature—boring and dumb literature.... It's interesting how the history of the subject works. Sociobiology was founded by Kropotkin. Nobody wants to know that because he drew conclusions from it that they don't like. He said, you know, that we're built for mutual aid in an anarchist society. So if that's your conclusion, we don't want your subject. There was no reverse engineering. He actually did it the right way; he was a natural historian. He recognized there is not much evolutionary evidence so he looked at the human evidence. Most of his work on mutual aid is a study of human society and elements of mutual aid that you find in them. So he thought it was reasonable to assume there is selection for this. So why isn't that called sociobiology or evolutionary psychology? Because it came to the wrong conclusion.[33]

M.W.: So basically the particular hypotheses that people spin about this are largely a reflection of their political ideologies?

N.C.: Sure. It's certainly not a reflection of anything that is understood in the sciences.

M.W.: So you think that the higher types of human behavior are simply mysteries?

N.C.: What I call a mystery is something that is outside the capacity of an organism. So it is a mystery relative to an organism. A lot of things that are mysteries to us are not mysteries to pigeons. You know, like pigeons can orient themselves in ways that humans can't. In fact, an insect can figure out where the sun is even if it can't see it just by using the time of the year and the time of the day. We can't do that. It's a mystery to us, but insects can do it.

The last word seems to be that it is an 'open question' whether we can or cannot attain reliable scientific knowledge about the biological bases of human knowledge and social behavior. The only way to answer this is to follow the scientific method we have. That is, lay out a sound program for research, select some interesting domains to study in detail, and attempt to develop some precise but initially inadequate theories, and push them to their limits in the hope of discovering where they go wrong. This is just what Chomsky and his linguistics students were doing in the late 1970s when a rather different approach to understanding language and language acquisition began to take shape.

THE MINIMALIST PROGRAM

In the Standard Theory of the 1960s and its variants, which are referred to as the Extended Standard Theory (ETS), there was a tension between the goals of linguistic theory of *descriptive adequacy* and *explanatory adequacy*. A grammar of a particular natural language was said to be descriptively adequate "to the extent that it correctly describes the intrinsic competence of the idealized native speaker," and a linguistic theory was said to be descriptively adequate "if it makes a descriptively adequate grammar available for each natural language" [ATS 24]. On the other hand, "to the extent that a linguistic theory succeeds in selecting a descriptively adequate grammar on the basis of primary linguistic data, we can say that it meets the condition of *explanatory adequacy*" [ATS 25]. To attain explanatory adequacy a linguistic theory would have to explain how the knowledge of his or her language that the native speaker acquires during the course of language learning was obtained "on the basis of an empirical hypothesis concerning the innate predisposition of the child to develop a certain kind of theory to deal with the evidence presented to him" [ATS 26]. He goes on to explain that at this time, (mid 1960s) the latter goal "would be utopian" and that "explanatory adequacy on a large scale is out of reach, for the present."

As research in linguistics progressed through the 'Chomskyan turn,' linguists began proposing a great many specific phrase structure and transformational rules for the various human languages they studied in an attempt to construct descriptively adequate grammars for each of them. But the more detailed and various these grammatical rules became, the more it seemed one had to complicate the picture of the LAD that was beginning to emerge, and "the goal of explanatory adequacy receded still further into the distance as generative systems were enriched in pursuit of descriptive adequacy, in radically different ways for different languages" [MP 5]. But a breakthrough came about in the early 1980s with the development of the Principle and Parameter (P&P) approach, X-bar theory, and the theories of government and binding. Even at an early stage of this development, in "Some Concepts and Consequences of the Theory of Government and Binding" (1982) Chomsky wrote that:

We hope that it will ultimately be possible to derive complex properties of particular natural languages, and even to determine the full core grammar of a language with all its empirical consequences, by setting parameters of general linguistic theory (universal grammar, UG) in one of the permissible ways. While this goal should always have been an obvious one, it is only quite recently that the task could actually be considered in a serious way, a development that is in my opinion a sign of significant progress in linguistic theory. [p. 3]

While the technical details of the P&P approach are beyond the scope of this book, I can give a sense of the basic idea.[34] All languages so far as we know have certain common principles that determine how the cases of nouns are treated (nominative, accusative, oblique), or that determine how pronouns are 'bound' to referring expressions in sentences, such as, *John washed his car*, where the pronoun *his* is bound to refer to whomever is referred to by *John*. But at the level of descriptive adequacy, the six thousand or so human languages seem to handle these problems in quite a number of different ways using what appear to be rather different principles. The P&P approach assumes that this variation can be accounted for by assuming that the LAD has a number of 'switches' that can be 'set' in different ways. Depending upon the primary linguistic data the child is exposed to, the switch will be set accordingly, and will yield different sets of basic grammatical rules for sentences in the language. At the deep and abstract level of UG, there are thought to be only quite general principles concerning phrase formation and movement of sentence elements, while the particular phrase structure and transformational rules proposed in grammars for individual languages are thought to be only taxonomic artifacts: "There are universal principles, and a finite array of options as to how they apply (parameters), but no language-particular rules and no grammatical constructions of the traditional sort within or across languages" (MP 6). The P&P approach suggested "a natural way to resolve the tension between descriptive and explanatory adequacy," since it both simplifies the presentation of descriptively adequate grammars for individual languages, while also providing a basis for seriously raising the sorts of questions about explanatory adequacy that Chomsky thought were utopian in 1965. Under the P&P approach, "it becomes the question of determining how values are set by experience for finitely many universal parameters, not a trivial problem by any means, but at least one that can be constructively pursued" [MP 7].

As this program progressed, "formulation of the P&P model led to

40

discovery and at least partial understanding of a vast range of new empirical materials, by now from a wide variety of typologically different languages," and to the realization that the early idea of a language-specific simplicity metric of some kind to evaluate the choice among grammars gives way to the deeper question about the *optimality* of a linguistic theory. Unlike the earlier notion of linguistic simplicity, the idea of optimality addresses the interface between the language faculty and other cognitive modules within the mind/brain system with which it must interact, namely the phonological [PHON] and semantic [SEM] systems:

> It appears that the computations of language have to be optimal, in a certain well-defined sense. Suppose we think of the process of constructing an expression as selection of words from the mental lexicon, combining them, and performing certain operations on the structures so formed, continuing until an expression is constructed with a sound and a meaning. It seems that some such processes are blocked, even if legitimate at each step, because others are more optimal. If so, a linguistic expression is not just a symbolic object constructed by the computational system, but rather an object constructed in an optimal fashion. [PP 28-29][35]

The search for the precise conditions for optimality has led to a whole series of 'hypotheses and refutations' about the nature of basic form of grammars and the possible principles and parameters of the LAD. As each new theory is proposed, it is tested against the known empirical facts, and evaluated against "general considerations of internal coherence, conceptual naturalness, and the like, 'simplicity,' in the external sense" [MP 9]. The goal is to get to a theory that is "minimal" in providing answers to two basic questions of linguistic research: "(1) what are the general conditions that the human language faculty should be expected to satisfy? And (2) to what extent is the language faculty determined by these conditions, without special structure that lies beyond them?" [MP 1].

CHOMSKY'S INTELLECTUAL LEGACY

The research program in linguistics and cognitive science that Chomsky launched is still going strong and is making progress in growing our understanding of this very difficult range of problems. As always, Chomsky is quite circumspect about claiming credit for these developments, or pronouncing them a success, though, undoubtedly, he had a major role in shaping the current directions of research in these fields. Since the 'Chomskyan turn' we have not been able to think of human beings on the model of rats running mazes, or pigeons pecking buttons for rewards, as psychological automatons whose behavior is easily explicable by means of simple-minded learning theories. Human beings are complex organisms with highly distinctive natures that determine, in detail, both our physical and mental attributes. There are plenty of things about our behavior that are quite mysterious, even to ourselves. It is possible to think that one day science will enable us to understand and explain who and what we are, and why we act in the ways that we do. But, we should not kid ourselves, Chomsky reminds us, into assuming that we presently possess that kind of deep and reliable theoretical knowledge about human nature. When one strips away all of the intellectual cant and posturing that hides our ignorance, one can only stand in awe and wonderment at the improbable fact that we exist, have been able to learn as much as we have about the world, about how to live with one another, and about how to construct the kind of technological civilization we have attained. Like Socrates who was said to be the wisest man of all in ancient Athens because he confessed his own ignorance, Noam Chomsky, has been wise about reminding us, more than two millennia later, that this is still largely the case, particularly as regards the Delphic problem of knowing ourselves.

But, he also reminds us that we should not give up hope for progress in human understanding. Primates we may be, but we can be damned clever ones. Perhaps this surprising cleverness – not only our ordinary creativity, but our remarkable capacity for discovery and invention, for doing science, producing art and music, and all of the 'higher' forms of human creativity – is the natural and universal basis of the intrinsic value we call 'human dignity'. If, as Kant thought, the intrinsic value of human lives is based on the possession of 'reason and conscience', it follows that social, economic, and political systems that stunt or stifle the human creative potential by means of illegitimate assaults on human freedom, security, and well-being, should be opposed, discredited, and in the end, dismantled in order to make room for humans beings to grow and to flourish. In each historical era, there have been serious threats to human dignity—slavery, racial discrimination, religious persecution, and sexism , to name a few--- threats that have had to be met and overcome through political struggle. The twentieth century was a particularly brutal one: wars, revolutions, and genocides took hundreds of millions of human lives. No genuine humanist, however devoted he might be to his professional career, could stand by passively and remain silent in the face of such injustice. Chomsky certainly did not.

3

CRITIQUES OF AMERICAN FOREIGN POLICY

And each form of government enacts laws with a view to it own advantage, a democracy democratic laws, and tyranny autocratic, and others likewise, and by so legislating they proclaim that the just for their subjects is that which is for their – the rulers' – advantage...This, then is what I understand as the identical principle of justice that obtains in all states – the advantage of the established government.

--Plato, *The Republic* Book 1

THE VIETNAM WAR

The 1960s was Chomsky's 'classic period.' In 1961, at age 33, he was made Professor of Foreign Languages and Linguistics at MIT. He and his wife Carol also began raising a family. Looking back on those times, Chomsky says, "Those were pretty hectic days. I was often giving many political talks a day all over the place, getting arrested, going to meetings about resistance and other things, teaching my classes, playing with the kids, etc. I even managed to plant a lot of shrubs and trees, somehow. Looking back, I can't imagine how it was possible."[36] As this quote indicates, Chomsky was, in addition to everything else, politically active during the 1960s, and soon became known as an outspoken critic of the U.S. war in Vietnam. Unlike most professors at elite universities in America, who shunned the student demonstrations of the 1960s, Chomsky joined them, gave numerous speeches, wrote articles for the *New York Review of Books* and other prestigious journals, and participated in teach-ins opposing the war.[37] For many, this was the first time they heard of this outspoken left-wing intellectual from MIT.

There was a spate of retrospective analyses of the Vietnam War during April 2000, marking the twenty-fifth anniversary of the fall of Saigon, and the end of the war America lost. Mainstream pundits now agree that the war was a 'mistake,' but draw out lessons that largely miss the point. Some say that it showed that "American should never enter a war it does not plan to win," or that, "We should not have gone into Indochina with one hand tied behind our back," or that the policy makers of the period "miscalculated the lasting appeal and viability of communism," or that they believed the nonsensical Domino Theory, or that Americans don't like seeing their sons come home in body bags, and are "unwilling to tolerate casualties." These sorts of points were never part of Chomsky's view; he criticized the U.S. war in Indochina because he thought it was immoral and illegal. He believes that the U.S. invasions of not only Vietnam, but Laos and Cambodia as well, during the 1960s and 1970s, were acts of aggression that constituted illegal interference in the affairs of other sovereign nations. In 1970 he wrote:

> Outside of the student movement, there is no substantial group that has taken a principled stand on the war. By this I refer to opposition to the war not on grounds of its costs, or failure, or remoteness from the national interest, or even its savagery, but rather opposition that is based on the same considerations that led to universal revulsion over the Russian invasion of Czechoslovakia:...I mean opposition based on the principle that no great power—not even one so selfless and beneficent as the United States—has the authority or the competence to determine by force the social and political structure of Vietnam or any other country, no right to serve as international judge and executioner. [PKF 85-86][38]

The Charter of the United Nations (1945) was designed to prevent the scourge of aggressive international war from recurring by placing strict legal limits on when nations may employ military force against other nations. It requires that the Security Council authorize all international measures, including the use of economic sanctions and blockades, as well as military action by land, sea, or air forces, (Arts. 41, 42), intended to respond to threats to peace and acts of aggression, save for measures taken immediately by Member States in self-defense (Art. 51). Chomsky takes this troublesome legal requirement to respect national sovereignty seriously, and from Vietnam through Kosovo has argued that the United States is in fact an 'outlaw state' since it has repeatedly disregarded this fundamental principle of international law whenever its leaders deem it expedient to do so.[39]

The idea that the government of South Vietnam 'invited' the United States to defoliate their forests, destroy their crops, bomb their towns and villages, and kill their people hardly merits serious consideration, any more than the idea that the people of Afghanistan 'invited' the Soviet Union to do the same for them in the early 1980s: "...as the London *Economist* recognized in the case of Afghanistan (but never in the case of Vietnam), 'an invader is an invader unless it is

44

invited in by a government with a claim to legitimacy,' and outside the world of Newspeak, the client regime established by the United States has no more legitimacy than the Afghan regime established by the USSR" [CR 225]. The only difference between these cases is that state propaganda in the United States has been more effective than its counterpart in the Soviet Union in convincing its own citizens that these aggressive wars were actually conducted for legitimate reasons of 'self-defense,' even though in neither case was the war fought on the soil of the nations seeking to defend themselves.

In a series of books, Chomsky presents a penetrating critique of the U.S. role in perpetrating aggression and supporting human rights violations in Indochina, Central and Latin America, in Turkey, Israel/Palestine, Pakistan, Iran, East Timor, Indonesia, Philippines, Korea, and elsewhere in the world. His tone is often ironic, (some might say sarcastic) with his moral outrage simmering only slightly beneath the surface of his prose.[40] In speaking about the so-called 'Vietnam Syndrome' that supposedly prevented the U.S. from sending American troops overseas following the debacle of the Vietnam War he wrote that it is:

> ...a disease with such ominous symptoms as opposition to aggression, terror, and violence and even sympathy for their victims. These 'sickly inhibitions against the use of military force,' as the symptoms were described by Reaganite intellectual Norman Podhoretz, were thought to have been cured by the glorious triumph over Grenada, when the United States was once again 'standing tall,' in the words of the president, after six thousand elite troops succeeded in overcoming the resistance of several dozen Cuban construction workers whom they had attacked and a few Grenadian militiamen, winning eight thousand medals of honor. [WOON 94]

This is the kind of remark that prompts many people to dismiss Chomsky as a left-wing wacko. But, if truth be told, as a direct consequence of U.S. aggression in Indochina, people are still dying in Vietnam, Laos, and Cambodia from mines and unexploded munitions dropped by U.S. forces more than a quarter of a century ago. Several millions of Vietnamese civilians died in the war and, even after it ended, thousands more bore children with grotesque birth defects, caused by the Agent Orange defoliants used by U.S. forces in an attempt to denude the forests that hid North Vietnamese convoys moving men and supplies down the Ho Chi Minh Trail to fight against the Americans. The U.S. government has never acknowledged its responsibility for civilian deaths it caused among the nearly three million Vietnamese who lost their lives in the struggle. It has never admitted that the war was illegal and immoral, nor that the pretexts that were invented for it, such as the Tonkin Gulf incident, were lies; and it has never apologized, accepted responsibility, or paid war reparations to the Southeast Asian countries American bombs destroyed. Mainstream commentaries instead focus on the tragic sacrifice of 58,000 American lives to a 'mistaken' war that we should have won, and think that the relevant lesson to be learned is that America should not enter a war that it does not have the will to win. Almost no one says that it was a case of U.S. aggression:

> For the past twenty-two years, I have been searching to find some reference in mainstream journalism or scholarship to an American invasion of South Vietnam in 1962 (or ever), or an American attack against South Vietnam, or American aggression in Indochina—without success. There is no such event in history. Rather, there is an American *defense* of South Vietnam against terrorists supported from the outside (namely, from Vietnam), a defense that was unwise, the doves maintain [CR 225].

Chomsky's careful and thorough dissection of the various lies, half-truths and distortions used by the U.S. government, the media, and academic apologists to disguise the true nature of the Vietnam War from the American people was the origin of what later became his 'propaganda model' of the American media and his theory of the 'manufacture of consent.' (See Chapter Four). Concerning his insistence that one rigorously apply contemporary standards in international law on human rights to U.S. foreign policy, Chomsky had this to say:

> N.C.: Internationally recognized human rights provide a useful standard – a useful working principle – for evaluating policy, domestic or international. But these are not the ultimate criteria, by any means. They reflect a level of moral consciousness that was achieved, though mostly on the

rhetorical level, in the past half century. A step forward, but surely not the final one, or anything like it. By even this minimal but useful standard, policy decisions should be harshly judged, in general. The U.S., for example, flatly rejects central components of the minimal international human rights system such as the UD.[41]

Chomsky may be alluding here to the fact that the U.S. Senate has failed to ratify the International Covenant on Economic, Social and Cultural Rights, one of the twin covenants comprising the International Bill of Rights which was based upon and derived from the Universal Declaration, as well as several other important international human rights treaties, such as the Convention on the Rights of the Child, which has been ratified by every country on Earth save for two – Somalia and the United States of America. But he may also be making the more general point that in case after case U.S. foreign policies have supported corrupt authoritarian regimes in other nations that systematically violate the human rights of their own citizens. The U.S. intervened in the internal affairs of other nations in the name of protecting vital 'national interests,' where that term is interpreted narrowly to mean the advantage of the established power, namely, the government of the United States and the U.S. business interests it represents. The United States has repeatedly violated the fundamental principle of the system of international law it helped to create in the shadow of the Second World War, namely that sovereign nations have the right to manage their own internal affairs without interference by other countries. According to Chomsky:

The U.S. has been radically opposed to international law since its modern foundations were established under U.S. initiative in 1945. In the early days, that was kept to internal (now declassified) documents, such as the first Memorandum of the newly-formed National Security Council (NSC 1/3), calling for military action in Italy if the left won the election ... With the Kennedy Administration, disdain for international law became quite public, in particular, in speeches by senior Kennedy adviser Dean Acheson. The main innovation of the Clinton/Reagan years is that it has become entirely open. In fact, the U.S. is the only country to have vetoed a Security Council resolution calling on all states to observe international law – mentioning no one, but everyone understood who was meant.[42]

American foreign policy, instead of adhering to nearly universally accepted principles of international law that afford weaker states at least some minimal protection against domination by their stronger neighbors, has generally followed the principle that 'might makes right.' Adherence to this principle is no where more evident than in U.S. policies towards its Central and Latin American neighbors.

CENTRAL AMERICA

A general pattern of U.S. support for regimes that systematically violate the human rights of their own citizens is nowhere clearer than in the case of U.S. policies regarding Nicaragua, El Salvador, Guatemala, Honduras, Colombia, Chile, and other Latin American countries. Chomsky says he agrees with Lars Schoultz, an academic specialist on U.S. policies towards Latin America, that the goal of these policies was "to destroy permanently a perceived threat to the existing structure of socio-economic privilege by eliminating the political participation of the numerical majority" [PP 96]. In particular, popular movements that aimed to redistribute land to impoverished peasants, to improve education and health care for the poor, and to distribute political power more democratically had to be defeated lest they set a 'bad example' by showing that such 'nationalistic regimes' of social and economic development responsive to the needs of the local population were in fact viable alternatives to corporate-driven capitalism. Chomsky documents in great detail these policies and their effects on the peoples of Central and Latin America. In the Preface to *The Culture of Terrorism* he wrote: "The central—and not very surprising—conclusion that emerges from the documentary and historical record is that U.S. international and security policy, rooted in the structure of power in the domestic society, has as its primary goal the preservation of what we may call 'the Fifth Freedom,' understood crudely but with a fair degree of accuracy as the freedom to rob, to exploit and to dominate, to undertake any course of action to ensure that existing privilege is protected and advanced" [CT 1].[43]

The modern history of American intervention in Central America began with the 1954 CIA-engineering coup that toppled Jacobo Arbenz, and led to a US-inspired counterinsurgency campaign in which U.S. trained and equipped paramilitary units 'disappeared' leftists, interrogated them under torture, and threw their bodies from helicopters into the sea. Throughout the 1970s and 1980s the United States continued to fund, instruct, and provide political support to the Guatemalan military, and by the end of the campaign in the 1990s, according to the UN Truth Commission, the death toll had amounted to nearly 200,000.[44] In El Salvador, a similar policy was begun under the Carter administration, expanded by President Reagan's 'activist' foreign policy into a program of state-sponsored terrorism directed against the population of the country carried out "by a U.S. mercenary army, trained, supplied, and directed by the United States" [CT26]. In an essay from 1982, Chomsky cites the report of a Congressional fact-finding mission in January 1981 whose members interviewed Salvadoran refugees along the Honduran border. They described atrocities they had witnessed including: "bombing and burning of villages by the army, mass murder of fleeing civilians, shooting of defenseless peasants from helicopters, and extraordinary brutality, e.g.,: mutilation; decapitation; children around the age of 8 being raped, and then they would take their bayonets and make mincemeat of them; the army would cut people up and put soap and coffee in their stomachs as a mocking. They would slit the stomach of a pregnant woman and take the child out, as if they were taking eggs out of an iguana. That is what I saw." When asked about the practices of the guerrillas, these informants said: "We don't complain about them at all. They haven't done any of those kinds of things. It's the military that is doing this. Only the military" [CR 340-341]. In El Salvador, the death toll in 1980 alone reached nearly 10,000; but by 1986, "The death toll under Reagan in El Salvador passed 50,000 and in Guatemala it may approach 100,000. In Nicaragua, the terror was less successful, amounting to only some 11,000 civilians killed under Reagan...." The reason for this discrepancy, Chomsky opined, was that "in Nicaragua the population has an army to defend itself from the U.S.-sponsored terrorist forces, whereas in El Salvador and Guatemala the terrorist force attacking the civilian population *is* the army" [CT 29].

Quoting secret National Security Council documents that laid out the rationale for these policies Chomsky reveals that successive American administrations from Truman through Reagan were concerned to protect American investments and trade in the region and to oppose "nationalistic regimes that are responsive to 'increasing popular demand' for immediate improvement in the low living standards of the masses" [CT 173]. To ensure that 'our resources' are not used to benefit the people of the countries in U.S.'s 'backyard,' it was thought to be necessary to 'gain 'predominant influence' over the Latin American military to ensure their understanding of, and orientation toward, U.S. objectives," namely the interests of U.S. corporations with investments in the region and the general interest in promoting export-oriented production from low-wage countries that keeps corporate profits high while also providing cheap consumer goods to Americans. The often-stated concern that Central America could be used as a staging base for Soviet-sponsored military aggression against the U.S. provided a plausible cover story to fool the gullible American masses, while also, incidentally, supporting another plank of the 'Reagan Doctrine' – "expanding the protected state market for high technology waste production and thus forcing a public subsidy to advanced sectors of industry; what is euphemistically called 'defense spending'" [CT 26]. But, the "primary root of U.S. interest in Latin America was 'the economic root' including investment and trade" [CT 173].

Nicaragua presented a troublesome case for the Reagan administration since up until the Sandinista Revolution in 1979, the U.S. had been able to rely on its puppet Somoza to look out for U.S. economic interests. Following Somoza's downfall, the Reagan Administration began a propaganda campaign in which it accused the Sandinista government of failing to meet its international obligations, press censorship, ill-treatment of the Miskito Indians, and even anti-Semitism, while 'Operation Truth' distorted the aims of the Sandinista Revolution by falsely claiming that they intended to "export revolution" to their neighbors [CT 219-221]. The Reagan Administration escalated this verbal assault into a full-scale guerrilla war conducted by surrogate forces known as the 'Contras' and then when Congress prohibited direct U.S. aid for the Contras (notorious for their human rights violations), carried on funding them secretly by means of the Iran-Israel arms deal engineered by Colonel Oliver North. The objective of U.S. policy was to "replace the Sandinista government by one more attuned to traditional U.S. standards for the region," and "to block and reverse social reform and diversion of resources to the needs of the poor majority...," and "to force Nicaragua to rely on the Soviet Union for survival and thus to provide retrospective justification for the attack launched against it for the crime of undertaking social reforms" [CT 27]. According to Chomsky, the U.S. accomplished this latter objective by denying an early Sandinista request for arms and training, blocking aid from international lending institutions, and pressuring its allies to do the same, thereby ensuring that "Nicaragua, lacking any other source, would become entirely dependent on Soviet arms," thus allowing the U.S. to justify the embargo it imposed (illegally in the judgment of the International Court of Justice which the U.S. spurned), against Nicaragua in 1986 as necessary to defend the hemisphere against Soviet imperialism.

While much of this program was a carefully guarded secret at the time, there was a significant amount of criticism of U.S. policies in

Central America from within the United States, a fact that Chomsky says, "was the essential factor that forced state terror underground in the 1980s, leading to problems when certain of its facets were exposed to a broad public during the [Iran-Contra] scandals of 1986" [CT 7]. For Chomsky, the silver lining in all of this is that these events demonstrate that "even in a largely de-politicized society such as the United States, with no political parties or opposition press beyond the narrow spectrum of the business-dominated consensus, it is possible for popular action to have a significant impact on policy, though indirectly" [CT 7].

But while the U.S. based Central American solidarity movement may have driven U.S. sponsored aggression under cover, it did not succeed in preventing the slaughter of hundreds of thousands of civilians by U.S. sponsored military and paramilitary forces. Writing in 1992, surveying the 'victory' of the United States in the Cold War against the Soviet Union and against 'communist subversion' in Central America, Chomsky summed up the results:

A decade later, the United States and its local allies could claim substantial success. The challenge to the traditional order was effectively contained. The misery of the vast majority has deepened, while the power of the military and the privileged sectors was enhanced behind a façade of democratic forms. Some 200,000 people had been killed. Countless others were maimed, tortured, 'disappeared,' driven from their homes. The people, the communities, the environment were devastated, possibly beyond repair. It was truly a grand victory. [DD 216]

But did the American public really learn any important lessons about their own government from this experience? The embarrassing facts revealed during Iran-Contra scandal were effectively covered up and soon forgotten, and Reagan's men were able to afford him a measure of 'plausible deniability,' thus thwarting his impeachment for the 'high crime' of directly violating a law passed by Congress. But as usual, important facts about the U.S. role in these tragedies were relegated to the 'memory hole,' and the important historical lessons about what the United States really stands for in world affairs were not drawn, at least not in the minds of the majority of Americans. For Chomsky, the important point was eloquently expressed by a murdered priest, Father Ignacio Ellacuría, Rector of the University of Central America, who was assassinated by elite government forces in San Salvador in November 1989. A few days before his death he addressed the issue of the underlying cause of the conflict in Central America, saying to a Western audience, "You have organized your lives around inhuman values." He said, these values, "are inhuman because they cannot be universalized. The system rests on a few using the majority of the resources, while the majority can't even cover their basic necessities. It is crucial to define a system of values and a norm of living that takes into account every human being." Chomsky continues with this comment: "In our dependencies, such thoughts are subversive and call forth the death squads. At home, they are sometimes piously voiced, then relegated to the ashcan in practice. Perhaps the last words of the murdered priest deserve a better fate" [DD 248].

INDONESIA AND EAST TIMOR

In Chomsky's view, the Indonesian invasion of the tiny former Portuguese colony of East Timor on December 7, 1975, "reveals with much clarity the hypocrisy of Western posturing about human rights, the utter fraudulence of the show of anguish over a certain well-defined class of terrible atrocities (namely those that are ideologically serviceable, since the perpetrators are official enemies), the causal acceptance of acts that would be described as genocidal were we not responsible for them, and the device of cloaking aggression in the guise of self-defense" [CR 303]. As in other cases, the story begins with a post-World War II plan to create a system of world order in which the under-developed countries of the Third World would function as a source of raw materials, cheap labor, and markets for the economies of the industrialized nations, led by the United States. When Indonesia, the world's fourth most populous nation, and also one that holds a strategic location straddling an important deep water channel between the Pacific and the Indian Oceans as well as oil reserves in the Timor Gap, seemed likely to upset this plan with nationalist ambitions, the CIA attempted, unsuccessfully, to overthrow President Sukarno in 1958, but then later succeeded in fomenting a military coup in 1965 that brought President Suharto to power, resulting in a bloodbath costing the lives of an estimated 500,000 people.[45] Suharto did, however, make Indonesia a welcoming place for U.S. investment, while he, his family, and his cronies profited richly from the deals that were struck, at least until popular, pro-democracy demonstrations led to his overthrow in 1998.

In 1974, citizens of East Timor led by the left-leaning nationalist party Fretilin attempted to exercise their right of national self-determination and win independence from their former Portuguese masters but were thwarted by the actions of the Indonesian military, which was, at that time as now, receiving the majority of its arms from the United States. When the Indonesian invasion came in 1975, the United States tried to give the impression of staying aloof, but "contrary to official lies, participated with enthusiasm" [CR 306]. "By 1977," writes Chomsky, "Indonesia had actually begun to exhaust its military supplies in this war against a country of 700,000 people, so the Carter administration took some time off from its pieties and self-acclaim about its devotion to human rights —'the soul of our foreign policy'—to arrange a large-scale increase in the flow of arms to Indonesia, in the certain knowledge that they would be used to consummate a massacre that was approaching genocidal proportions" [CR 306]. By 1979, the war had cost the lives of an estimated 200,000 East Timorese and had reduced the country to rubble. The Indonesian occupation of East Timor, which was almost immediately declared illegal by the United Nations, continued until 1999, when an internationally supervised election allowed the East Timorese people to vote on whether they wished to be independent. They did, overwhelmingly, but that did not prevent a renewed round of atrocities by militias equipped and run by the Indonesian Army from wreaking havoc in the period leading up to and immediately following the referendum.[46] During our interview in April 2000, I asked Chomsky whether he thought that U.S. policy towards East Timor had changed:

N.C.: There is no evidence that the U.S. has changed its position.... The fact is that the U.S. supported Indonesia right through the end of the atrocities. It wasn't until after the atrocities were consummated, in mid-September, finally Clinton told them to call it off. It was over. There was never any attempt to do a thing. In fact they blocked it. Did you see any air drops to starving people?

M.W.: Australia did something.

N.C.: East Timor saved Australia from Japanese invasion and they lost 40,000 people protecting a couple hundred Australian commandos in the 1940s. You know they don't teach about this in the schools there, but the people know about it. People have an uncle or grandfather. It's part of the culture. The idea that East Timorese died to protect us from the Japanese, and now we are selling them out to the Indonesians, that didn't sit very well.

Chomsky cites the U.S. backed Indonesian invasion of East Timor in 1975 as a prime case showing the selectivity of reporting of the corporate media and the establishment intellectuals. The case presents as close as one gets to a controlled experiment to test the adequacy of his propaganda model of the U.S. media (See Chapter Four), since on April 17, 1975 the Khmer Rouge of Cambodia captured Phnom Penh, ushering in the darkest period of that country's dismal modern history, leading to an 'auto-genocide' that took the lives of 2 million people. During the same fateful year, on April 30, 1975, the forces of North Vietnam took control of Saigon (renamed Ho Chi Minh City), thus ending the Vietnam War. An analysis of the column inches in major American newspapers at the time devoted to coverage of the massacres in Cambodia and those in East Timor, reveals, according to Chomsky, that the American media "required no instructions from the State Department 'to cut down reporting from Timor'". In the *New York Times,* for example, "coverage of Timorese issues had been substantial in 1975, but declined as Indonesia invaded and reduced to zero as the atrocities reached their peak...," while at the same time, the Western press was "consumed with agony and outrage over the atrocities in Cambodia under the Khmer Rouge" [CR 306-307]. Chomsky accounts for this discrepancy by noting that the crucial difference between the two cases was that, "in the case of Cambodia, the outrage was ideologically serviceable and hence intense," but, nevertheless, "no one suggested any way to bring the atrocities to an end," while, in East Timor, "the silence was crucial":

> It was of critical importance to ensure that the public was unaware of what was happening so that there would be no impediment to the ongoing slaughter. To bring the atrocities [in East Timor] to an end required no intervention; it would have sufficed to call off the hounds. The example provides much insight into the nature of the Western conscience and its moral concerns.... [CR 310]

Also largely unreported at the time was the U.S. role in creating the conditions for the Khmer Rouge take-over in Cambodia: the U.S. invasion of that country in April 1970, the vicious U.S. bombing campaign that followed, and then the callous abandonment of the weak government of U.S. puppet Lon Nol in 1973, leading to its ultimate collapse in 1975.[47] Despite the fact that the U.S. government denounced the atrocities committed by the Khmer Rouge (while doing nothing to try to stop them), when the carnage was finally ended by a

Vietnamese invasion in January of 1979, the U.S. decided that the Democratic Kampuchea coalition, led by the ousted Khmer Rouge, would receive U.S. recognition at the United Nations as the sole 'legitimate government' of Cambodia. In the eyes of U.S. policymakers, Vietnamese occupation of Cambodia was a worse crime than the Khmer Rouge genocide that it ended. Chomsky sardonically comments that by 1980 "the 'inconsistency' between our opposition to Khmer Rouge massacres and support for comparable Indonesian massacres" had been overcome, "since the United States now supports both Pol Pot and the Indonesian murderers" [CR 311]. The moral of this suppressed story, as in other cases that Chomsky has helped bring to light, is that "we live under the rule of force, not the rule of law, in the sense that the great powers do what they choose, as do others if they can get away with it, irrespective of the law and high-sounding principles" [PP 205-206]. In practice, the UN Charter provisions prohibiting aggression are worthless when US interests are involved.

ISRAEL/PALESTINE

Chomsky is fond of quoting a remark made by President George Bush following the U.S. victory over Saddam Hussein in the Persian Gulf War in which he boasted that dictators and tyrants know that "What we say goes," as an usually honest admission of the way things are. Chomsky has written thousands of pages of commentary and analysis on the twists and turns of the Israel/Palestine conflict, continually updating his views as events have unfolded, and providing extensive documentation for his analysis.[48] While I cannot possibly do justice to this vast amount of material here, I do want to give an overview of the main elements of his perspective.

According to Chomsky, the central goal of U.S. policy in the Middle East has been and is to establish U.S. control over the strategically important oil reserves that lie beneath the Arabian peninsula, what the State Department has described as "probably the richest economic prize in the world" [WOON 190]. America's actions in the Middle East over the past half century, from the CIA-engineered coup against Mossadegh of Iran in 1953, to U.S. support for a 'Sparta Israel,' to U.S. support for Saddam Hussein's repression of the Kurds in Iraq, to the present U.S. sponsored sanctions against Iraq, have been conditioned and directed by this overarching goal. The strategy for securing this prize was to transfer the spoils of British imperialism into U.S. hands while "recognizing that direct colonial rule was no longer possible" [WOON 198]. The solution was to create a façade that would

' "consist of family dictatorships that do what they are told, and ensure the flow of profits to the United States, its British client, and their energy corporations." U.S. interests in the region are to be protected by "regional enforcers, preferably non-Arab (Turkey, Israel, Iran under the Shah, Pakistan)," but "British and U.S. muscle stand in reserve, with military bases from the Azores through North Africa to the Indian Ocean and the Pacific" [WOON 198]. The primary threats to be avoided were Arab 'economic nationalism' and 'social democracy' that might entail attempts by the people of the region to take control of their own resources and deny the U.S. and Britain access to the cheap oil they needed to keep their economies humming.

The special relationship between the U.S. and Israel developed within this general strategic context. Impressed by Israeli military prowess, first against the British in the 1948 War of Independence (or what the Arabs call 'al Naqba'– the catastrophe), and then again in 1967, 1973, and 1982, the United States has come to view its number one recipient of foreign aid as a reliable regional enforcer and as the central pillar of its overall regional strategy: "The U.S.-Israel alliance has been based primarily on the perception of Israel as a 'strategic asset' fulfilling U.S. goals in the region in tacit alliance with the Arab Façade in the Gulf and other regional protectors" [WOON 206]. But the Palestinian/Israeli conflict has been an ongoing problem threatening regional 'stability' and so has had to be addressed.

Chomsky's version of this struggle is considerably different from the official version served up by the U.S. media, so it is important to understand at the outset the assumptions that form the basis of his approach: "The first of these is the principle that Israeli Jews and Palestinian Arabs are human beings with human rights, equal rights; more specifically, they have essentially equal rights within the territory of the former Palestine. Each group has a valid right to national self-determination in this territory. Furthermore, I will assume that the State of Israel within its pre-1967 borders, had and retains, whatever one regards as the valid rights of any state within the existing international system" [CR 372]. He goes on to explain that the term 'rejectionism' is standardly used to refer to the position of those "who deny the existence of the State of Israel, or who deny that Jews have the right of national self-determination within the former Palestine," a view that he denies. However, he also condemns the "racist assumption that Jews have certain intrinsic rights that Arabs lack," and so, when he uses the term 'rejectionism' he intends it to be taken in an inclusive sense to encompass also the views of those who "deny the right of national self-determination to Palestinian Arabs." Based on this egalitarian sense of 'rejectionism,' Chomsky charges that beginning in 1948 and continuing

56

after the end of the 1967 war to the present, U.S.-Israeli rejectionism has blocked the achievement of a viable and comprehensive settlement of the conflict that recognizes the equal rights to national self-determination of both Israeli Jews and Palestinian Arabs.

Another basis for Chomsky's position is the international consensus represented by UN Resolution 242 of 1967 which required that Israel return virtually all the land it conquered in the 1967 war in return for a guarantee of secure borders and other measures designed to ensure peace in the region – i.e., 'land for peace.' According to Chomsky the fulfillment of 242 has been consistently thwarted by Israel's refusal, supported by the U.S., to return to its pre-1967 borders. This policy has, however, gone through several stages. Here is a somewhat telescoped version of Chomsky's basic account. From 1967 to 1973 the U.S. publicly supported 242, for instance in the Rogers Plan of 1969, but secretly pursued a rejectionist position, advocated by Henry Kissinger, under which there would be a 'Greater Israel' serving as a U.S. strategic asset in the conflict prone, but oil rich, Middle East. When Egyptian President Anwar Sadat essentially accepted 242 in February 1971, and "offered Israel a full peace treaty on the pre-June 1967 borders, with security guarantees, recognized borders, and so on," he called the bluff and so caused a panic in Israel which promptly rejected the offer and stepped up its settlement program in the occupied territories to continue 'building facts' that would impede any eventual return of the lands it had taken by force. In 1972, Israel also rejected the proposal by King Hussein of Jordan to establish a confederation of Jordan and the West Bank by asserting Israeli sovereignty over Judea and Samaria (the Biblical names the religious rejectionists within Israel give to the West Bank). Sadat had repeatedly warned that he would be forced to resort to war if his attempts at a peaceful settlement were rebuffed, and so, in 1973 "he decided to try a limited military option which, combined with an oil embargo, would lead to a significant Israeli withdrawal from Arab territories" [CR 393]. While Israel quickly prevailed militarily, when Saudi Arabia joined Egypt and Syria in the oil boycott—"the first major use of the 'oil weapon,' a move with considerable long-term implications for international affairs"— Washington realized that "Egypt and the oil-producing states could not be so easily dismissed or controlled" and shifted its strategy [CR 394]. Now the goal would be "to accept Egypt as a U.S. client state" thus removing it from the conflict, while allowing Israel to go forward with its policies of integrating the occupied territories into Greater Israel. During this phase, both Israel and the United States refused to recognize the Palestinians as legitimate negotiating partners and refused to meet with the PLO, dismissing it as a 'terrorist organization.'

The U.S. also made it clear that it did not want the Europeans or the Soviets interfering with U.S. prerogatives, and more than once used its veto in the Security Council to ensure that a peace settlement under the terms of UN 242 would not be struck.

When Anwar Sadat made his historic journey to Jerusalem in November 1977, he was acclaimed by the American media as having finally seen the light by accepting Israel's right to exist. But Sadat had already accepted this in principle in 1971, so it became important to expunge the pre-1977 record of his earlier peace initiatives that Israel and the U.S. had rejected. The Camp David Peace Accords in 1978 advanced several U.S. strategic objectives: they ensured that the Europeans and the Soviets were excluded from the diplomatic arena; they isolated the Palestinians, enabling Israel to consolidate its hold over the West Bank and Gaza; and they removed Egypt and Jordan from the conflict, thus breaking up the Arab united front and allowing Israel to deal separately with its Northern enemies, Syria and the PLO in Lebanon. This Israel proceeded to do, first with its 1978 and again with its 1982 invasions of Southern Lebanon. According to Chomsky, "The actual reasons for the 1982 invasion have never been concealed in Israel, though they are rated 'X' in the United States" [WOON 214]. As Prime Minister Shamir later stated, (Chomsky quoting him), "Israel went to war because there was a 'terrible danger...Not so much a military one as a political one," namely that, by observing the cease-fire and appearing to prefer negotiations to terrorism, the PLO "was gaining respectability" and was beginning to appear as a legitimate negotiating partner. Chomsky notes, that "all of this is completely falsified in what reaches the American public," with the official story that the Israeli invasion was to protect the civilian population in the North from Palestinian rockets and artillery, an outcome that was never achieved, even after Israel withdrew to its present (but soon to be ended) security zone, and the enemy changed from the 'reformed' PLO to Hezbollah.[49]

The Intifada upset U.S. and Israeli plans for a continued stalemate in peace negotiations because it forced the Israelis to appear as brutal oppressors. Popular resistance propelled international consensus to accept a moderated and weakened (some would say compromised) PLO as the legitimate representative of the aspirations of the Palestinian people and to move towards something superficially resembling the 'two state' solution that had been envisioned as early as 1948, but which has been consistently opposed by the U.S. and Israel. In attempting to manage this latest phase of the conflict, the U.S. position was considerably strengthened by the Persian Gulf War:

After the Gulf war, Europe accepted the US position that the Monroe Doctrine effectively extends over the Middle East; Europeans would henceforth refrain from independent initiatives, limiting themselves to helping implement US rejectionist doctrine, as Norway indeed did in 1993. The Soviet Union was gone from the scene, its remnants now loyal clients of Washington. The UN had become virtually a US agency. Whatever space the superpower conflict had left for nonalignment was gone, and the catastrophe of capitalism that swept the traditional colonial domains of the West in the 1980s left the Third World mired in general despair, disciplined by forces of the managed market. With Arab nationalism dealt yet another crushing blow by Saddam's aggression and terror and PLO tactics of more than the usual ineptitude, the Arab rulers had less need than before to respond to popular pressures with pro-Palestinian gestures. The U.S. was therefore in a good position to advance its rejectionist program without interference, moving towards the solution outlined by Secretary of State James Baker well before the Gulf crisis: any settlement must be based on the 1989 plan of the government of Israel, which flatly bars Palestinian national rights.[50]

The intended goal of the present policy "is to ensure Israel's control of the territories, with scattered cantons of local Palestinian administration" that will resemble South African 'Bantustans' except for the fact that the latter were subsidized by South Africa, "while the U.S./ Israeli plan is to leave the Palestinian cantons the task of dealing with the bitter effects of the military occupation, which barred any possibility of economic development."[51] In fact, the Israeli economy is very dependent on the cheap labor supplied by the Palestinians, just as the white South Africans were dependent on the impoverished black workers. This solution was acceptable to Yasser Arafat, who having sold out his people for personal power, came to be seen as someone the U.S. and the Israelis could do business with. The 1993 agreement signed by Israel and Arafat sold out Palestinian rights to national self-determination in exchange for a 'limited autonomy arrangement' under which the Palestinians are given autonomy to manage their own affairs under Israeli supervision, with the Palestinian Authority serving as the enforcer necessary to keep the unruly masses in line, thus removing the Israeli military from its direct role in maintaining repression. The best outcome, from Washington's point of view, "would be a settlement that entrenches the traditional strategic conception and gives it a public form, raising tacit understandings to a formal treaty. If some

59

arrangement for 'local autonomy' can resolve the Palestinian issue, well and good. Meanwhile security arrangements among Israel, Turkey, Egypt and the U.S. can be extended, perhaps bringing others in if they accept the client role."[52] The human rights of the Palestinians have always been of secondary concern to U.S. policy makers who have acted in this as in other cases primarily in order to protect the sacred right of American corporations to pump oil.

KOSOVO

On March 24, 1999, NATO forces led by the U.S. and Britain began bombing Serbia. The announced purpose of the bombing campaign was to stop a vicious program of ethnic cleansing being conducted by the army and paramilitary units of the Federal Republic of Yugoslavia (FRY) against the majority Muslim Albanian population of Kosovo. NATO's action was hailed as 'a landmark in international relations' and indicative of a 'New Humanism' in American foreign policy in which "the brutal repression of whole ethnic groups will no longer be tolerated," leaving "those responsible for such crimes...nowhere to hide" [NMH 2]. The bombing campaign ended on June 3 after the Kosovo Peace Accord was accepted by NATO and Serbia. A great victory for the forces of truth and goodness was declared and the thousands of Kosovar refugees who had fled their homes during the bombing campaign to seek safety in UNHCR refugee camps in neighboring countries began to return to their burnt out and bombed out homes and villages under the watchful eye of a NATO-led occupation force. Almost before the smoke had cleared, Chomsky published a scathing critique of NATO's only war.

In *The New Military Humanism: Lessons from Kosovo*, Chomsky uses his familiar intellectual weapons, a relentless rationalism combined with an astonishing grasp of the (often hidden) facts of the matter to test the claim that NATO's military campaign was carried out for primarily humanitarian reasons. He begins his analysis by reminding us of several 'moral truisms:'

> The first is that people are primarily responsible for the likely consequences of their own actions, or inaction. The second is that the concern for moral issues (crimes, etc.) should vary in accordance with ability to have an effect (though that is not of course the only factor). A corollary is that responsibility

mounts the greater the opportunities and the more free one is to act without serious cost. Accordingly, responsibility is far greater for privileged people in more free societies than for those lacking privilege or facing severe penalties for honesty and moral integrity. [NMH 39]

Chomsky says he does not question the claim that Slobodan Milosevic, the President of the FRY, who, during the 1990s, led his people into three disastrous and losing wars against the break-away provinces of Croatia, Bosnia, and finally Kosovo, has been guilty of numerous and heinous crimes. The question he asks is whether the response of the U.S., the U.K. and their NATO allies to the situation in Kosovo in early 1999 was not also a crime, rather than the noble humanitarian crusade it was portrayed to be in the media.

He notes that in any humanitarian crisis involving war crimes or massive human rights violations there are three possible actions that bystanders (that is, the people who are neither the perpetrators nor the victims of the crimes in question), can undertake, "(I) act to escalate the catastrophe, (II) do nothing, (III) try to mitigate the catastrophe" (NMH 48). Near the end of his book he reaches the following conclusion:

> A reasonable judgment, I think, is that the U.S. chose a course of action that – as anticipated – would escalate atrocities and violence; that strikes yet another blow against the regime of international law, which offers the weak at least some limited protection from predatory states; that undermines democratic developments within Yugoslavia, possibly Macedonia as well; and that sets back the prospects for disarmament and for some control of nuclear weapons and other weapons of mass destruction, indeed may leave others with "no choice" but to "obtain weapons of mass destruction" in self-defense. Of the three logically possible options, it chose (I) "act to escalate the catastrophe," rejecting the alternatives: (II) "do nothing," (III) "try to mitigate the catastrophe." [NMH 155]

Rather than representing a departure from past policies, the "new internationalism replays old and unpleasant records," in which the world's only superpower, acting as the global policeman, along with its faithful sidekick the Former Empire (a.k.a. Great Britain), ignored the UN Charter's provisions on the authorized use of force, and initiated a pusillanimous high altitude bombing campaign against Serbia simply because they 'believed it to be just.'

Chomsky quotes Robert Hayden's claim that, "the casualties among Serb civilians in the first three weeks of the war are higher than all of the casualties on both sides in Kosovo in the three months that led up to the war, and yet those three months were supposed to be a humanitarian catastrophe" [NHM 20].[53] In Chomsky's view, NATO's bombing campaign was as if, "...you see a crime in the streets, and feel that you just can't stand by silently, so you pick up an assault rifle and kill everyone involved: criminal, victim, bystanders," what he elsewhere calls the 'Carthaginian solution' [NMH 156].

During the year preceding the bombing campaign, the U.N. Security Council had issued a series of warnings to the FRY to desist in its 'anti-terrorism' campaign against the Kosovar Liberation Army (KLA), each of which ended with the threat to invoke the provisions of the Charter under Chapter 7 which would authorize member states to employ force to meet threats to international peace and security. In January 1999, a massacre was committed in the Kosovar village of Racak in which some 45 persons were allegedly killed by paramilitary forces under the control of the FRY. The event received extensive coverage in the major media and was later claimed to have been the decisive turning point at which the allies began preparing for a military campaign. However, there was still a diplomatic effort under way in the form of negotiations in the French town of Rambouillet among the U.S., its NATO allies, the FRY, and the OSCE which had positioned a volunteer force of observers in Kosovo in an attempt to monitor human rights violations and prevent more violence. But these monitors were ordered to withdraw shortly before the bombing campaign commenced, and the Rambouillet talks broke down when, according to the official version, Serbia refused to accept the 'reasonable terms' presented in the proposed agreement, leaving the 'enlightened nations' no choice but to resort to military force to end the FRY's vicious campaign of ethnic cleansing and to prevent 'another Bosnia.'

Chomsky notes that "the Terms of the (Rambouillet) agreement were not made available to the general public," and that to understand what really happened "it is important to find out what they were" [NMH 106]. Quoting portions of the (rejected) Interim Agreement for Peace and Self-Government in Kosovo that was privately circulated on the internet (See Chapter Five "The Diplomatic Record" note 6 [NMH 178]). He reveals that the Rambouillet Agreement called for "complete military occupation and substantial political control of Kosovo by NATO, which regards Kosovo as a province of the FRY, and effective military occupation of the rest of the FRY at NATO's will" (NMH 106). The crucial paragraph concerning the occupation of Serbia is

> 8. NATO personnel shall enjoy, together with their vehicles, vessels, aircraft, and equipment, free and unrestricted passage and unimpeded access throughout the FRY including associated airspace and territorial waters. This shall include, but not be limited to, the right of bivouac, maneuver, billet, and utilization of any areas or facilities as required for support, training, and operations. [NMH 107]

Chomsky says, "It has been speculated that the wording was designed so as to guarantee rejection. Perhaps so. It is hard to imagine that any country would consider such terms except in the form of unconditional surrender." The Serbian National Assembly did, predictably, reject these terms on March 23, and called for the OSCE and the UN to facilitate a diplomatic solution. But the U.S./U.K. and their NATO allies rejected this course and chose to initiate the bombing campaign.

According to Chomsky, the political leadership in Washington and London must surely have anticipated that bombing Serbia would cause the FRY to escalate its atrocities against the defenseless civilian population of Kosovo, which it did, leading to the deaths of thousands and to a massive refugee flow. However, in typical fashion, once the bombing was well underway NATO publicists tried to portray the escalation of atrocities within Kosovo as having been planned before the bombing commenced, under a nefarious scheme dubbed 'Operation Horseshoe'. This was a convenient cover-up: "The culpability of Clinton, Blair, and their associates would pass beyond astonishing ignorance to extreme criminality if indeed they knew (as they now claim) that huge atrocities were underway or about to occur while doing nothing whatsoever to prepare for the flood of refugees they anticipated. And the criminality mounts still higher if they failed to notify Commanding General Wesley Clark, as he maintains" [NMH 36]. A month after the NATO bombing campaign began General Clark reported to the press that the plans for Operation Horseshoe "have never been shared with me," and that NATO's operation,

> ...was not designed as a means of blocking Serb ethnic cleansing. It was not designed as a means of waging war against the Serb and MUP forces in Kosovo. Not in any way. There was never any intent to do that. That was not the idea.

If this testimony is not regarded as sufficient rebuttal to the claim that NATO's only war – which was, incidentally, self-servingly dubbed 'Operation Just Cause'—was carried out for 'humanitarian reasons,' there are, Chomsky goes on to argue, "elementary ways to test the thesis that is pronounced with such authority and solemnity: ask how the same enlightened states behave elsewhere" [NMH 38], particularly in cases when faced, "with comparable or worse atrocities that they could reduce or terminate easily and costlessly, merely by withdrawing their participation in them" [NMH 48].

Drawing on the historical record on U.S. military support for Colombia, where during 1999 human rights NGOs and even the U.S. State Department reported between 2,000 and 3,000 people massacred or extrajudicially executed, most of them by the Colombian military and associated paramilitary units, Chomsky notes that, rather than acting to mitigate the catastrophe, U.S. military aid to Colombia was slated to increase dramatically in 1999 (and again in 2000) under the pretext that it was needed to fight the 'drug trade' and a Communist insurgency [NMH 49-51]. Similarly, NATO member Turkey has been carrying out what amounts to a vicious campaign of 'ethnic cleansing' against its minority Kurdish populations for decades, while Washington has done nothing to prevent it, but the U.S. has instead consistently authorized the sale of M-60 tanks, F-16 fighter-bombers, Cobra gunships, Blackhawk helicopters and other advanced U.S.made military equipment to the government of Turkey, equipment that has been shown by Amnesty International to have been used to commit human rights violations against the Kurds [NMH 51-62].[54] Chomsky notes that, "Though the atrocities (in these cases) fall well within the designated time frame, and indeed continue right now, they do not bear on the principles of the New Humanism:" Since the atrocities are being committed in these cases by 'our friends' they must instead be expedited [NMH 62]. Charges of a 'double standard' are, he says, "quite wrong: 'our values' are implemented with no slight inconsistency" [NMH 57]. Nor is there any basis for believing that Kosovo represents a departure from past policy and practice which has been one in which the world's 'rogue superpower' resorts to force whenever its feels that its security or economic interests are threatened.

If the bombing of Serbia was not done to prevent ethnic cleansing, then what was the motive? According to Chomsky's analysis,

Throughout the crisis, NATO leaders emphasized, with general agreement, that the decision to bomb on March 24 was obligatory for two reasons: (1) to stop the violent ethnic cleansing that the NATO bombing precipitated, as anticipated; and (2) to establish "the credibility of NATO." The first reason we may put aside, but the second is plausible. [NMH 134]

After quoting a variety of elite opinion-makers who publicly supported the view that preserving NATO's credibility as it approached its fiftieth anniversary on April 1, 1999 was the real reason for the bombing campaign against Serbia. Chomsky supplies his own translation of such pronouncements:

> When Clinton, Blair and the others speak of the "credibility of NATO," they are not expressing their concern about the credibility of Italy or Norway: rather of the reigning Super-power and its attack dog. The meaning of "credibility" can be explained by any Mafia Don. When a storekeeper does not pay protection money, the goons who are dispatched do not simply take the money: they leave him a broken wreck, so that others will get the message. Global Mafia Dons reason the same way, and understandably so. [NMH 135-136]

Recalcitrants such as Slobodan Milosevic and Saddam Hussein are not being punished for their human rights violations and other crimes, rather for their refusal to conform to Washington's demands. The basic policy has been in place since 1917 when the Soviet Union was perceived as 'setting a bad example,' but America's policy direction was given further legitimacy by the 'Kennedy intellectuals' who saw Castro as a 'bad example,' a 'rotten apple' who might 'spoil the barrel,' in America's 'backyard' by successfully charting a course independent of Washington's control. So they planned and carried out the (unsuccessful) Bay of Pigs invasion and then the subsequent total economic embargo against Cuba. In keeping with the U.S. policy of punishing non-conformist nations that insist on their own economic and political sovereignty, "As long as Serbia is not incorporated within the U.S.-dominated domains, it makes sense to punish it for failure to conform – very visibly, in a way that will serve as a warning to others that might be similarly inclined" [NMH 137].

Besides the direct toll of the bombing campaign in civilian casualties, both Kosovar and Serbian, NATO's campaign also deepened the distrust of Russia and China of U.S./U.K. motives and undermined the most important principle of international law: the UN

Charter provisions that restrict the use of force in the international arena only to cases of self-defense or to those authorized by the UN Security Council to respond to threats to international peace and security (Chapter 7). The U.S. did not even attempt to gain Security Council authorization for the NATO bombing, no doubt expecting that Russia, and perhaps China, would cast vetoes against it and urge that the diplomatic alternative be pursued. Instead, the U.S. and the U.K simply ignored the UN Charter, following a consistent pattern of disdain for international law, when it does not suit their interests. The fact that the bombing was 'extra-Charter' and hence illegal, was rarely mentioned in the U.S. media, but it created considerable anxiety among the 'unimportant nations' such as India, whose major national newspapers were highly critical of the NATO operation condemning it as "characterized by illegality, self-interest, arrogance, and lawlessness," and opining that the U.S. has become "the rogue state par excellence repeatedly defying international rulings whether by the World Court or by UN resolutions when these have not suited its interests" [NMH 143]. It is not surprising, therefore, that much of the world perceives what the U.S. and NATO did as granting itself the 'license for world-wide interventionism,' particularly in cases where it can hide its real policies under the cloak of humanitarianism.

But Chomsky's critics will not easily be convinced that what NATO did in Kosovo was simply another act of U.S. aggression. How do you intervene to stop ethnic cleansing somewhere in the world if one of the permanent members of the Security Council powers can stop it for its own sectarian reasons? For all of its merits, the UN is a deeply flawed institution, and no feature of the present UN system is more flawed that the Security Council with its five permanent members able to block any action through the use of the veto. The U.S. regularly uses its veto to block any action against Israel. Russia had indicated that it would use its veto to block any UN action against Serbia. NATO, which also includes nations like Canada, the Netherlands, Italy and Germany, that do not regularly flout international law, was confronted with a genuine moral dilemma: They could either stand by passively obeying the letter of international law as ethnic-cleansing was allowed to proceed unimpeded in southern Europe, or they could bypass the Security Council and act to try to prevent it. NATO decided to act in this case, after giving a great deal of time, (perhaps too much time) to the diplomatic process. Then, weighing the odds, decided that it simply would be immoral and inhuman to turn a blind eye to the destruction of a people in Europe. Perhaps the NATO planners did anticipate FRY reprisals against the Kosovars, but they also seemed to have believed that the resort to force by a united NATO would lead to a quick capitulation by Serbia. They were wrong about that latter assumption, as it turned out, but they cannot be faulted for trying to derail a human rights catastrophe. When I challenged Chomsky on this point he had this to say:

> N.C.: They didn't know for sure, but we know they expected it. Clark, the NATO commander, informed the press the day the bombing began that it is entirely predictable that there would be an escalation in atrocities. They knew it was very likely.

> M.W.: But they figured once they started bombing Milosevic would cave.

> N.C.: Let's suppose that's true. Does that justify it? No. What was going on before? I don't think it was so clear when I wrote the book, but now there is a huge amount of documentation available about what was going on in Kosovo before the NATO bombing began. The Pentagon, the OSCE, NATO have all done studies to try to bolster the case for the bombing. But the documentation totally destroys their case. What it shows is that nothing much was going on. The typical cycle was that KLA commandos would attack (from across the border incidentally) and kill some Serbian policemen and civilians, then the Serbs would mount a disproportionate response, which they (the KLA) were trying to get. Then another attack. So, yeah, the Serbian responses were disproportionate, but nowhere near as bad as say what Israel's does or what we do, for instance. So what's the point of bombing? Even if they believed they were going to cave in. What it does is just establish U.S. control. Furthermore, if you want to carry out military action you have to meet a heavy burden of proof. The fact that I'm not certain that it might make things worse is not an argument. By that you can you can justify just about anything. So I think this thing was proven to be completely criminal.

The subsequent events in Chechnya and the comparatively weak U.S. and NATO response to them seem to bear out the main points of his analysis. When it comes to the U.S. acting to halt ethnic-cleansing, what matters most is whether our 'friends' are doing it.

CHOMSKY'S ETHICS

What emerges from these various critiques of American foreign policy is the view that nations, even powerful nations like the United States of America, need to apply a moral yardstick to their own actions in the international arena. Might, after all, does not make right, however much the political realists who have fashioned U.S. policies would like to convince us it does. At least the realists are not hypocrites about recommending the use of U.S. power to protect and advance our national interests, however narrowly these are defined. But in a democratic society one needs to place the naked reality of power politics behind a façade of moral respectability to gain popular support for the preferred policies of elites who formulate U.S. foreign policy. Chomsky quotes Reinhold Niebuhr as having remarked that, "perhaps the most significant moral characteristic of the nation is hypocrisy":

> The point is well taken. There is a simple measure of hypocrisy, which we properly apply to our enemies. When peace groups, government figures, media, and loyal intellectuals in the Soviet sphere deplore brutal and repressive acts of the United States and its clients, we test their sincerity by asking what they say about their own responsibilities. Upon ascertaining the answer, we dismiss their condemnations, however accurate, as the sheerest hypocrisy. Minimal honesty requires that we apply the same standard to ourselves. [NI 123]

Chomsky's critiques of the U.S. have been largely motivated by this desire to be honest about the role of the U.S. in world affairs during the past fifty years. The moral yardstick he employs is not all that radical. It consist of relatively straightforward ethical assumptions like: one should not commit aggression upon other countries; one should not attempt to interfere with their internal affairs; one should not attempt to steal the natural resources of other peoples; one should not commit or support the commission of human rights violations; one should obey international human rights and humanitarian laws (such as the Geneva Conventions and the Universal Declaration of Human Rights); one should treat similar cases similarly and different cases dissimilarly; one should try to prevent harm or at least to mitigate harm when it is in one's power to do so; if one wrongfully causes harm to others (for instance by dropping bombs on them), one should compensate the victims; one should not lie about what one is doing; one should take responsibility for the effects of one's own actions, and similar sorts of commonsense moral principles.

When we met, I asked him whether he had an ethical theory from which he derived his moral assumptions:

N.C.: Like a hundred percent of the rest of the species, I have no ethical theory. Do you know of an ethical theory that applies to the questions we have been discussing? Ethical theories are way too hard. They are just hard problems. We have some understanding; we have moral intuitions. You can kind of organize them. You can find a few principles that are valid as truisms. You can call it an ethical theory if you want, but the word 'theory' doesn't really apply. . . . Pragmatists just say, you know, do what works. The utilitarians – first of all it collapses into such vagueness, you know, what do you mean by good? So it dissolves right away. Kant is an interesting thinker, the categorical imperative: "Treat people as ends in themselves rather than as means only." But they are truisms when you spell them out, and they don't help you when you are dealing with real circumstances.

Like much of Chomsky's thought, this is a refreshing honest admission of ignorance. As a Cartesian, Chomsky believes there is such a thing as 'moral common sense,' that provides a reasonably reliable guide to moral judgment for most people. Perhaps there is even something like a 'moral competence' analogous to linguistic competence, that we rely upon to inform our ordinary moral judgments and actions, that we 'know' implicitly more or less as we 'know' the rules of our language.[55] But for the LT(H,D) that concerns this particular kind of human knowledge we call morality, we lack any detailed and descriptively adequate characterization of exactly what is known in the final state, our moral competence. We can use this knowledge to make moral judgments, but we don't really have a scientific theory about it, how it developed, and what its biological roots in our brains might be. Not having a good scientific theory about ourselves, we have to muddle through as best we can. And we do, especially when we at least try to be minimally rational and honest about making moral judgments, particularly about our own behavior, which is the one kind of behavior we can directly control. By extension, citizens of democratic societies who have at least some measure of control over their government's policies and actions, and so are more responsible for those policies and actions than are citizens of authoritarian states. When those policies and actions are unethical, citizens need to speak out and try to change them. This is basically what Chomsky has tried to do.

4

CHOMSKY'S POLITICAL PHILOSOPHY

Pay no attention to the man behind the curtain.

--L. Frank Baum. *The Wizard of Oz*

DEMOCRATIC IDEALISM

Chomsky's political criticism is often dismissed as representing the ravings of a 'self-hating Jew' (when he is criticizing Israel), or a 'disloyal American' (when he attacks U.S. foreign policies). He is frequently mischaracterized by the corporate media as an 'ultra-liberal' or a Marxist, but he is none of these things. He describes his own political philosophy as 'libertarian socialism' or as a form of 'anarchosyndicalism,' but these terms are unfamiliar and are likely to be misunderstood. As a social critic, he is clearly deeply committed to what can be called 'democratic idealism,' the really quite radical view that ordinary people are quite capable of governing themselves if they are freed from the interference of false political ideologies imposed upon them by dominant systems of power. If anything, Chomsky is a 'radical democrat' since he believes in the traditional Enlightenment (and quintessentially American) ideals of individual liberty, democratic self-determination, and human rights. He is, however, dismayed by the way in which America has strayed from these original Enlightenment ideals in its pursuit of power and profit. Much of his political writing is designed to reveal the contours of the system of unaccountable corporate-controlled political power created by and for the 'rich men who rule the world' and to encourage popular resistance to its continued domination in both domestic and foreign affairs.

Chomsky is an example of a particular kind of 'internal' critic of modern American political culture that is nicely characterized by the following passage by Michael Walzer:

Despite the difficulty, we can clearly see readily enough how a critique of American politics could be developed from [a] thick account of democratic idealism. The critique would have a twofold focus. It would aim first at exposing the most important kind of distributive aggression in American society: the invasion of the political sphere by wealthy individuals or by the masters of corporate wealth.... The power of wealth is certainly characteristic of contemporary America—and because it is characteristic, it has its own ideological justifications. So the democratic idea must be articulated with these in mind, against them, showing in specific ways with concrete examples, how state power is seized and even used though the consent of those subject to it is never asked. Democratic criticism would aim, secondly, at revising the internal boundaries of American society—exposing the exercise of something very much like political power outside the recognized political sphere, beyond the reach of the principle of consent. Here there are a number of different targets, each with its own ideological defenses, which need to be addressed one by one: the despotism of factory managers and corporate executives, the autocracy of university presidents, the patriarchal absolutism of male 'heads of households,' and so on.[56]

Chomsky has spent a great deal of time and much effort in addressing some of these significant targets and dismantling their ideological defenses by means of closely reasoned arguments based on facts and a remarkable grasp of broad trends in the historical record. He does not often miss the forest for the trees. But Chomsky's political philosophy is 'anti-ideological' – he has no 'system of thought' or 'political theory' that he claims is based on any deep theory of human nature, and repeatedly warns against such views on the grounds that, "Surely our understanding of the nature of man as of the range of viable social forms is so rudimentary that any far-reaching doctrines must be treated with great skepticism," particularly, "when we hear that 'human nature' or 'the demands of efficiency' or the 'complexity of modern life' requires this or that form of oppression and autocratic rule" [FRS 152]. Rather he advocates a fluid and pragmatic program of social change whose goal is to "search for ways to liberate the creative impulse, not to establish new forms of authority" [PKF 54].

The previous political philosophers he seems to admire most are anarchist thinkers such as Mikhail Bakunin and Rudolf Rocker. He began his introduction to Daniel Guerin's *Anarchism: From Theory to Practice* with a quote from Rocker that seems to come close to expressing his own view:

> Anarchism is not a fixed, self-enclosed social system but rather a definite trend in the historic development of mankind, which, in contrast with the intellectual guardianship of all clerical and governmental institutions, strives for the free, unhindered unfolding of all the individual and social forces in life....For the anarchist, freedom is not an abstract philosophical concept, but the vital concrete possibility for every human being to bring to full development all the powers, capacities, and talents with which nature has endowed him, and turn them to social account. [FRS 151]

He goes on in this essay to contrast libertarian socialism, which seeks the dissolution of centralized authority whether of powerful governments or powerful corporations and the devolution of power to individuals in consensual communities, with authoritarian socialism, that is, Leninism and Maoism, which sought to conquer and control political and economic power and transfer them to an elite party apparatus. Chomsky rejects all forms of undemocratic authoritarianism, both 'state communism' and 'state capitalism,' in favor of a vision of 'democratic control in the workplace and the community that he calls 'anarchosyndicalism' or 'libertarian socialism'. Chomsky's brand of libertarianism should not be confused with the classical liberalism of John Locke, which is now sometimes also referred to as 'right libertarianism.' Right-libertarians place emphasis on the inviolability of property rights, since they believe that private property, by which Locke had meant primarily land, is a necessary means for defending one's life and liberty. Right libertarians nowadays oppose state intervention in social and economic life to allow for free and unlimited accumulation of property and wealth by individuals and private corporations. Chomsky clearly rejects this ideal, noting that,

> It is true that classical libertarian thought is opposed to state intervention in social life, as a consequence of deeper assumptions about the human need for liberty, diversity, and free association. On the same assumptions, capitalist relations of production, wage labor, competitiveness, the ideology of 'possessive individualism' – all must be regarded as fundamentally anti-human. Libertarian socialism is properly to

be regarded as the inheritor of the liberal ideals of the Enlightenment. [FRS 157]

The Enlightenment ideals that Chomsky speaks of are those of pre-capitalist eighteenth century thinkers such as Adam Smith, who he says were "guided by sympathy and feelings of solidarity with the need [of workers] for the control of their own work" [CW 20]. Adam Smith might seem an unlikely hero for Chomsky, but that is only because most people have not actually read his classic *The Wealth of Nations* (1776). While everyone knows his ideas about of the division of labor and the 'invisible hand' of the market, not many people, "get to the point hundreds of pages later, where he says that the division of labor will destroy human beings and turn them into creatures as stupid and ignorant as it is possible for a human being to be" [CS 20]. While Smith favored 'free markets' (under conditions of perfect liberty), he did not believe that England in his day had anything close to 'perfect liberty'. He worried about the growing ability of the 'merchants and manufacturers' of England to control state policies, and he harshly criticized British colonial policies, such as those in India. Twentieth century right-wing economic libertarians, such as F. A. von Hayek, and the neoliberal economists of the Chicago School don't mention Smith's worries about how entrenched power imbalances effect the so-called 'free market.' Instead, they seek to prevent the state from interfering with corporate control over virtually all aspects of economic life and the continued domination of American politics by business elites. This is basically the political function of the Republican Party. Bill Clinton and his fellow 'New Democrats,' have resigned themselves to corporate control and seek to use state power in order to lightly regulate the corporate-dominated economy, to modestly redistribute wealth to the poor, to protect a little of what's left of the natural environment, and to protect workers from some of the worst abuses of the concentrated economic power of big corporations. They seek to mitigate some of the social and environmental harm caused by untrammeled capitalism, never challenging the basic system of corporate rule.

But for libertarian socialists or democratic idealists like Chomsky, neither domination by private capital nor regulation by a powerful central state is the solution to the problem of securing human freedom. The long-term solution lies in the direction of dismantling all systems of concentrated power (both private and public) and devolving effective control over most economic and political decisions to the people whose lives are most effected by those decisions. Chomsky rejects the necessity implied by the slogan, "Democracy stops at the factory gates," and like, Bertrand Russell, whose views he admires on this subject, Chomsky envisions a society in which "the men who do the work in a business also control its management" [PKF 61]. "Socialism," he says, "will be achieved only insofar as all social institutions, in particular the central industrial, commercial, and financial institutions of a modern society, are placed under democratic control..." Put another way, all the stakeholders in an enterprise, that is, all those whose interests are affected by its decisions should have a voice and a role in making those decisions. But, concerning the major political and economic institutions of the contemporary world order, we are still far from realizing this ideal:

> Russell's general approach to this range of topics seems to me eminently reasonable, and—after half a century of tragedy—as remote as ever from any likelihood of achievement. 'The real obstacles,' Russell thought, 'lie in the heart of man, and the cure for these is a firm hope, informed and fortified by thought.' Perhaps, in some sense, this is true. But the obstacles are immense and the means for overcoming them still slight and frail. [PKF 62]

Following the collapse of the Soviet Union and the end of the Cold War in 1989-1991, state capitalism led by the United States and the other members of the G-7 has become an even stronger force in world affairs. The recognition that this is the case has spawned a movement within global civil society to try to make large corporations more accountable to society, to 'put a human face' on corporate-led globalization. Getting the state to provide a democratically-accountable counter-balance to corporate power may be a short-term goal. However, the ultimate goal of left libertarians and anarchists is not a strong state; rather it is the eventual dismantling of all systems of centralized and unaccountable power; the devolution of authority and control over the primary political and economic organs of society to the people themselves who are the ultimate sovereigns in classical democratic theory. The core of Chomsky's political philosophy is a form of radical democratic idealism, the really revolutionary idea – to paraphrase Lincoln's famous formulation – that governments should be 'by, for, and of the people,' not 'by, for, and of corporations.'

Chomsky believes that the original democratic ideals of the Enlightenment have been systematically subverted in America by the rise, during the latter half of the nineteenth century, of the modern corporation, leading to a transformation of the American political system into the form of government he calls 'state capitalism' but which others sometimes call 'plutocracy' – rule by the wealthy. The seeds for this development were, according to Chomsky, already present in the thought and works of several of the Founding Fathers, particularly, the Federalists who wanted to ensure that the new republic would be governed by the 'men of best quality' and who saw to it that the U.S. Constitution was written, in the formulation of John Jay and James Madison, so as to "protect the minority of the opulent against the majority" [PP 47]. This was accomplished not only by completely disenfranchising women, blacks, and American Indians, but also by effectively barring 'landless men' from political participation by means of state property qualifications for voting.[57] The fifty-five men who gathered in Philadelphia in the summer of 1787 were for the most part wealthy landowners who wanted to protect their own economic interests, and who feared popular movements of the poor, such as Shay's rebellion (1786-1787), in which small farmers in Western Massachusetts rose up to protest debt burdens that enabled the new government to expropriate their small family farms. The men of property, however, included not only large landowners, but also the emerging class of wealthy industrialists, what de Tocqueville later called 'the manufacturing aristocracy', who were creating the Industrial Revolution in America. Alexander Hamilton, the first Secretary of the Treasury, believed that the economic future of the new republic would rise with the interests of this manufacturing class, and made plans to extend credit and raise tariffs to protect America's fledgling industries, (i.e., what are now called 'protectionist' measures that the U.S. now opposes when they are erected by other countries to protect their developing economies). Such moves were opposed by democrats, among others, Thomas Jefferson, who, in his later years,

...drew a distinction between 'aristocrats' and 'democrats'. The 'aristocrats' are 'those who fear and distrust the people and wish to draw all powers from them into the hands of the higher classes'. The democrats, in contrast, 'identify with the people, have confidence in them, cherish and consider them as the honest & safe depository of the public interest', if not always the most wise'. The aristocrats of his day were the advocates of the rising capitalist state, which Jefferson regarded with dismay, recognizing the obvious contradiction between democracy and capitalism—or more accurately, 'really existing capitalism', linked closely to state power [PP 88].

But, just as Jefferson had feared, during the nineteenth century the power of corporations and the capitalist aristocracy steadily increased. Federal and state court decisions encouraged the growth of limited liability corporations, which granted shareholders freedom from personal responsibility for their company's debts. At the same time states were granting more and more corporate charters, and state legislatures were investing large amounts of public money in the construction of canals, railroads, highways, and other public infrastructures that were of great economic benefit to the manufacturers and merchants. Through such public subsidies to businesses, a partnership developed between the state and private capital that characterizes the particularly American form of capitalist democracy that Chomsky calls 'state capitalism'. According to one historian, "By the middle of the nineteenth century the legal system had been reshaped to the advantage of the men of commerce and industry, at the expense of the farmers, workers, consumers, and other less powerful groups within society...."[58] In the latter half of the nineteenth century, the U.S. Supreme Court ruled that corporations were 'legal persons' and that therefore, like real persons, (i.e., human beings), they could claim constitutional protection under the Fourteenth Amendment, implying that they could not be deprived of their property without due process of law, thus limiting the ability of states to effectively regulate them. Of the Fourteenth amendment cases argued before the Supreme Court between the years 1890 and 1910, "19 dealt with the Negro, 288 dealt with corporations."[59] The American democratic experiment evolved in more or less the way Karl Marx had predicted; the government pretended to be neutral and represent the interests of the 'people' while in fact it was increasingly functioning as the 'executive committee of the bourgeoisie' making sure that no matter who happened to hold political power, the interests of capital would be protected. It is essentially this system of 'private tyrannies' functioning under the official protection of the state that persists in America to the present day, though, of course, it has grown much richer and more powerful.

THE 'NEW' WORLD ORDER

In the twentieth century, sometimes referred to as 'The American Century', the American "industrial-financial-commercial sector, concentrated and interlinked, highly class conscious, and increasingly transnational in the scope of its planning, management, and operations," extended its influence overseas in order to make the world safe for American corporate capitalism [WOON 1]. Of course, the politicians did not say this. Instead, America's crusade in the First World War was portrayed as a struggle to 'make the world safe for democracy,' which makes sense, according to Chomsky, if you mean

'American-style democracy' that is, "a political system with regular elections but no serious challenge to business rule..." [DD 331]. On the other hand, if by 'democracy' you mean a system of government in which "citizens may play some meaningful part in the management of public affairs," then, "the United States has no principled opposition to democratic forms, as long as the climate for business operations is preserved;...it is only when this is threatened by what is regularly called 'Communism' that action is taken to "restore democracy" [NI 111]. All this makes sense in American Orwell-speak, "when we take the term 'democracy' to mean domination of the economy and social and political life by domestic elements that are properly sensitive to the needs of corporations" [NI 108].

President Woodrow Wilson, who is mainly remembered for his Fourteen Points, his rhetorical support for the doctrine of national self-determination, and for his role in creating the League of Nations, also ordered invasions of Haiti and the Dominican Republic that, "killed thousands, restored virtual slavery in Haiti, and dismantled its parliamentary system because legislators refused to accept a 'progressive' constitution written in Washington that allowed U.S. investors to turn the country into their private plantation...;" [PP 97]. The largely suppressed history of American imperialism continued to evolve through the end of the Second World War, despite the domestic political setbacks to corporate domination brought about by the Great Depression and Roosevelt's New Deal. After the Second World War, the United States emerged as the pre-eminent world power, and recognizing this fact, U.S. policy-makers hastened to develop a plan designed to ensure that American global military and economic hegemony would be protected and extended in the Post-War era.

> The underlying assumption is that there is a stable international order that the United States must defend. The general contours of this international order were developed by U.S. planners during and after World War II. Recognizing the extraordinary scale of U.S. power, they proposed to construct a global system that the United States would dominate and within which U.S. business interests would thrive. As much of the world as possible would constitute a Grand Area, as it was called, which would be subordinated to the needs of the U.S. economy. Within the Grand Area, other capitalist societies would be encouraged to develop, but without protective devices that

would interfere with U.S. prerogatives. In particular, only the United States would be permitted to dominate regional systems. The United States moved to take effective control of world energy production and to organize a world system in which its various components would fulfill their functions as industrial centers, as markets and sources of raw materials, or as dependent states pursuing their 'regional interests' with the 'overall framework of order' managed by the United States. [NI 25]

Within this general framework, the Marshall Plan was designed to help the defeated industrial powers, Japan and Germany, rebuild their economies and states on the American corporate capitalist model. The 'socialist' countries, the Soviet Union and the People's Republic of China, were viewed as mortal threats to American business and security interests that had to be 'contained' and so the Cold War commenced. In the economic arena the neo-liberal trade and monetary policies that form the present 'Washington Consensus' represent a retreat from the 'liberal' international economic system set up by the victorious powers at the end of the Second World War. When first introduced, U.S. policy planners recognized the need to provide smaller nations with protection against the market and capital power of the more powerful nations. The IMF's initial mandate was to provide short-term loans to stabilize currencies, but it has since expanded into providing long-term loans with conditions attached that force borrowing countries to remove tariffs and dismantle social programs. These conditions, known as structural-adjustment programs or SAPs, require borrowers to cut subsidies for such basic government services as education, health care, and food, to privatize state property, to raise interest rates to attract international investors, and to lower barriers against foreign ownership of the country's assets. The World Bank's original job was to make long-term loans, and, historically, it has emphasized investments in large infrastructure projects such as roads, bridges, power plants, dams and industrialized agriculture, rather than social programs. Western corporations whose governments contribute to both of these funds get the contracts to build these projects, so the money loaned is really a disguised form of corporate welfare, while the people of the developing countries are left holding the debts that were mainly incurred by corrupt oligarchs in their own governments who skimmed off their shares of the Western largesse to pad their own secret Swiss bank accounts.

The Bretton Woods institutions, the World Bank, and the International Monetary Fund (IMF), were created on the assumption that the Post-war world would be characterized by 'free trade' but 'regulated capital.' But the major thrust of the neo-liberal economic policy reforms introduced in the 1970s was to remove all possibility of imposing regulations on both trade and the movement of capital by trading nations. The reason why American corporations wanted these regulations removed, according to Chomsky, is because "regulation of capital would allow governments to carry out monetary and tax policies and to sustain full employment and social programs without fear of capital flight" [PP 150]. Neo-liberal economists, who Chomsky regards as essentially academic apologists for corporate domination of the world economy, were not happy with such restrictions, and beginning with the Nixon Administration's decision to move the U.S. off the gold standard, began to dismantle the safeguards built into the Bretton Woods system designed to defend the economically weak from the capital power of the economically strong. In the 1990s, we saw the results. Without controls on the movement of capital across national borders, and with the advent of the internet-powered electronic transactions, a 'virtual senate' of currency speculators can "impose its own social policies on reluctant populations, punishing governments that deviate by capital flight," [PP 150] as was witnessed, for instance, in 1997 with the Asian economic crisis whose epicenter was Thailand.

The popular struggles in the 1990s over the failed Multilateral Agreement on Investment (MAI), the demonstrations around the World Trade Organization (WTO) meeting in Seattle in November 1999, and the demonstrations in Washington DC in April 2000 around the annual meetings of the World Bank and the IMF, however, signal that popular resistance to these policies is forming. Understanding of and resistance to corporate domination of the global economy is growing, and it may yet succeed in creating a more just and democratic international economic order once a sufficient number of people are able to 'look behind the curtain' to see what the princes of commerce and their political allies have really been doing.

Chomsky acknowledges that even in a reformed international economic order there should be a role for corporations to protect their interests; but he thinks the interests of capital need to be balanced by other voices with competing interests at the table. As it presently stands, everyone except corporate interests are excluded, and the real workings of this system of power are hidden from view of the general population. This lack of transparency, of course, is just what the rich men who rule the world want: "Putting it in plain terms, the general public must be reduced to its traditional apathy and obedience, and driven from the arena of political debate and action, if democracy is to survive" [NI 3]. The anti-corporate domination protesters in Seattle and D.C. are a small minority of Americans who, working in solidarity with colleagues from the developing world who represent the people of those countries, not their elites, continue to hold onto the notion that what they think should matter to those who hold the reins of power. The demonstrations against the World Bank and the IMF in Washington on April 16th 2000, took place just a couple of days before I had my face-time with Noam, so I asked him this question:

M.W.: Some of the demonstrators were saying that the World Bank should be shut down. Do you believe the World Bank should be shut down? And if it were to be shut down, what would replace it?

N.C.: I don't think it should just be shut down. If you shut it down it would be a catastrophe. I don't think corporations ought to exist. They are illegitimate. But if you just shut them down it is a catastrophe. I mean, I don't think Bolshevism should have existed, but to shut it down was a catastrophe. To shut down the Bolshevik system meant killing millions of people. Which is what happened. Look at death rates in the 90s [in the Former Soviet Union]; it has been out of sight. You shut down an illegitimate system you can just cause a catastrophe. Because society is integrated, it works in a certain way. You can't just take one piece of it and say, OK I'll wipe this out and somehow the rest will continue to work. It won't.

M.W.: So you have to reform it?

N.C.: Yeah. Diversify the system and let it be some subpart that reflects a particular interest which interacts with others like the ILO which has every right to be part of the system, and bring in concerns of the Indian peasants and people who are worrying about whether the next generation will be able to survive, environmentalists, and so on. There is no legitimacy to organizing the whole system around one issue – how can you maximize profits for private tyrannies....So it's a good organizing slogan, but you have to think about it....But, the whole series of protests starting with the MAI, and Seattle and so forth, has been very encouraging.

It is rather remarkable that as many people participated in these demonstrations as did, since "apart from educated elites, much of the population appears to regard the government as an instrument of power beyond their influence and control" [NI 4]. There are, in fact, quite a number of 'attentive citizens' who take an active interest in keeping themselves informed about world affairs and current policy debates, but not the so-called 'silent majority.'

THE MANUFACTURE OF CONSENT

Why don't most Americans bother to vote? Why does the majority remain 'silent' and not attempt to participate in the development of U.S. foreign or domestic policy? Why don't more people demand that their government behave ethically in its dealings with other nations? Chomsky's answer to these questions, and the feature of his political philosophy for which he is probably best known, is his critique of the corporate media, and in particular, his views concerning 'thought control in democratic societies.'

Chomsky did not coin the term 'the manufacture of consent;' he attributes it to the journalist Walter Lippman who used it to describe a 'revolution' that would transform the practice of democracy [CR 136]. A similar notion, the 'engineering of consent', came from Edward Bernays, one of the founders of the public relations industry. In Chomsky's view, in state capitalist societies that are nominally democratic, such as the U.S., the ruling elites understand that it is necessary to reduce the general public to apathy and obedience and to mislead them about the real reasons behind political decisions. Here is how Chomsky describes the concept of democratic systems of thought control in contrast with the obvious and unsophisticated methods used by totalitarian states:

> In the democratic system, the necessary illusions cannot be imposed by force. Rather, they must be instilled in the public mind by more subtle means. A totalitarian state can be satisfied with lesser degrees of allegiance to required truths. It is sufficient that people obey; what they think is of secondary concern. But in a democratic political order, there is always the danger that independent thought might be translated into political action, so it is important to eliminate the threat at its root [NI 48].

Chomsky's 'propaganda model' of the U.S. media does not presuppose that there is a literal conspiracy to hide and distort the truth; rather he argues that self-censorship operates systematically at an institutional level within the major media. The main techniques are the omission of facts that would be embarrassing to the state religion, and the narrowing of public debate to a range of 'thinkable' and 'moderate' alternatives all of which support the 'religion of state capitalism.'

It is necessary to establish a framework for possible thought that is constrained within the principles of the state religion. These need not be asserted; it is better that they be presupposed, as the unstated framework for thinkable thought. The critics reinforce this system by tacitly accepting these doctrines, and confining their critique to tactical questions that arise within them. To achieve respectability, to be admitted to the debate, they must accept without question or inquiry the fundamental doctrine that the state is benevolent, governed by the loftiest intentions, adopting a defensive stance, not an actor in world affairs but only reacting to the crimes of others, sometimes unwisely because of personal failures, naiveté, the complexity of history or an inability to comprehend the evil nature of our enemies....This is a system of thought control that was not perceived by Orwell and is never understood by dictators who fail to comprehend the utility for indoctrination of permitting a class of critics who denounce the errors and failings of the leadership while tacitly adopting the crucial premises of the state religion. [CR 132]

In addition to suppressing evidence and only allowing 'responsible' criticism well within the bounds of 'acceptable thought' into the 'marketplace of ideas', the 'opinion-shapers' also rewrite the historical record by "creating and entrenching highly selective, reshaped or completely fabricated memories of the past" [CR 124]. Pundits distort present realities by using Orwellian doublespeak, in which, for instance, American aggression in Central America is called 'defensive' and American rejection of a real two-state solution in for Israel/Palestine is called the 'peace process'. What one gets in the news, especially TV news, is an assortment of platitudes marking the range of 'acceptable opinion', filled with 'emotionally potent oversimplifications' recited during seven minute stretches between commercials. This kind of selective reporting about the past or present actions of the U.S. government is "a valuable mechanism of control, since it effectively blocks any understanding of what is happening in the world."

A great deal of Chomsky's political writing can be seen as an attempt to correct this selective and distorted portrayal of American policies at home and abroad, and to give his readers the suppressed facts that support a truer picture of the behavior of the world's only superpower. For most readers, the voluminous factual documentation he provides will be surprising and instructive, but for many the unflattering picture he paints of American policies may provoke shock and disbelief. Most people who read Chomsky say they find his ideas provocative, but that they don't agree with them. This is to be expected if, as he claims, most Americans have been thoroughly indoctrinated by the media in the tenets of the state religion. The state religion holds that the U.S. is never the aggressor (it is always resisting aggression); that atrocities and human rights violations are committed by our 'enemies,' never our 'friends,' who are merely defending themselves against terrorism; and that people in other countries are yearning for the American-style 'freedom' and 'democracy' and so it is our nation's noble purpose to promote these values around the world. In fact, the real objective of American foreign policy is to make the world safe of U.S. corporations, and to give them the ability to make money by moving capital and products anywhere they choose; the "U.S. system is one political party, with two factions controlled by shifting segments of the business community" [NI 22]. The corporate media's role is to inform the American public of the current divisions among the elites, but it rarely calls into question their dominance over public discourse, since making too much of that would shatter the 'necessary illusion' that the people, not the state-corporate elites, are actually running the country.

Like Chomsky, John Dewey worried about the growing control over popular consciousness by the corporate media, and urged an inquiry "concerning the necessary effect of the present economic system upon the whole system of publicity; upon the judgment of what news is, upon the selection and elimination of material that is published, upon the treatment of news in both editorial and news columns" [WOON 89]. But since Dewey's time, the problem has only gotten worse. The views of the upper classes, and particularly the corporations, dominate the American media, and consequently the 'marketplace of ideas' available to most Americans. In the 1990s, the era of corporate mega-mergers, the global media have come to be dominated by nine mega-corporations: Time Warner (CNN), Disney (ABC), Bertelsman, Viacom, News Corporation (FOX), TCI, General Electric (NBC), Sony (Columbia Pictures), and Seagrams (Universal Studios).[60] Many of these large media firms have some of the same major shareholders, own pieces of one another, or have interlocking boards of directors. These media corporations are in the business of delivering a product, namely audiences, to their advertisers, which are, of course, other corporations:

In short, the major media—particularly the elite media that set the agenda that others generally follow—are corporations 'selling' privileged audiences to other businesses. It would hardly come as a surprise if the picture of the world they present were to reflect the perspectives and interests of the sellers, the buyers, and the product. [NI 8]

The corporate dominance of the media functions in a systematic, structural way to select the news and information that is made available to the general population. The result is accomplished not through secret deals in smoky rooms, but simply because many independent decision-makers are operating with the same worldview, under the same values, and with the same basic goal – to turn a profit for their corporate parents. The corporate-controlled media behave rather like a school of fish (some might say sharks), that can wheel and turn in unison without there being any plan guiding their behavior, only the scent of blood and a sensitivity to the needs of the corporate hands that feed them. He provides examples of how projects that are deemed unsuitable for corporate sponsorship 'die on the vine,' how, for instance, TV stations engage in self-censorship in order to protect their advertising revenue, and how those few journalists who have the courage to buck the system are weeded out. The influence of advertisers on content is often indirect. "Projects unsuitable for corporate sponsorship tend to die on the vine," but sometimes, according to a London Economist article on Gulf+Western's reaction to WNET's airing of a documentary called "Hunger for Profit, " it can be quite direct. In this case, Gulf's CEO wrote to this public TV station saying that airing this program, which had depicted greedy multinationals buying up farm land in the third world, was 'virulently anti-business' if not 'Anti-American.' Gulf later withdrew its corporate underwriting from the station. "Most people believe that WNET would not make the same mistake today." Those who rise to managerial positions in the major media understand these realities, and, in fact, "belong to the same privileged elites, and might be expected to share the perceptions, aspirations, and attitudes of their associates, reflecting their own class interests as well. Journalists entering the system are unlikely to make their way unless they conform to these ideological pressures, generally by internalizing the values;...and those who fail to conform will tend to be weeded out by familiar mechanisms" [NI 8].

Increasingly, there is little real news of any kind on television, the medium through which most Americans get their news. What is mainly broadcast nowadays is 'infotainment' designed to motivate mass consumption of movies, fashions, cosmetics, luxury vacations and whatever else is currently for sale, and to nourish the 'cult of celebrity' that mainly celebrates the hyper-consumption life-styles of the rich and famous. This kind of 'soft news' is sandwiched into seven-minute slots between the commercials, which are, after all, the real reason for the broadcast. According to Chomsky, the goal of the mass media is to lull the ignorant masses into political apathy. They do this by creating pleasing distractions – consumerist fantasies, attachment to meaningless professional sports, and grossly oversimplified and distorted versions of contemporary events – thereby inducing a 'philosophy of futility' and lack of purpose in life, by concentrating attention on the more superficial things that comprise much of fashionable consumption. If that can be done, then people "will accept the meaningless and subordinate lives that are appropriate for them and they'll forget subversive ideas about taking control of their own lives."[61] In performing this function, the "media are vigilant guardians protecting privilege from the threat of public understanding and participation" [NI 14]. By creating the 'national entertainment state' they distract the masses from paying too close attention to what is being decided on their behalves. Whenever popular awareness does break out of these confines, the mainstream media can be relied upon to distort and misrepresent what the protest was all about, as was the case with the popular demonstrations in November 1999 at the WTO meetings in Seattle. The mainstream press labeled the protesters as miscreants and 'Flat-Earthers' who were opposed to globalization and 'free trade'. In order to find any more accurate account of what really happened in Seattle, and why, one needed to go to the so-called alternative press.[62]

Given the corporation domination of the major media, it is not surprising that most people are ill-informed about world events and about the real nature of the system of power led by the United States. But what about the members of educated elites? Chomsky reserves his deepest scorn and his most biting sarcasm for his fellow intellectuals, often other distinguished professors at major research universities, who willingly and faithfully serve the interests of concentrated state-corporate power. This strand of Chomsky's work was already evident in his 1966 article "The Responsibility of Intellectuals" in which he took on academic apologists who defended U.S. policies in Vietnam [CR 59-82]. A famous Chomsky quote comes from that article: "It is the responsibility of intellectuals to speak the truth and to expose lies." In many of his later writings he extended his attack against thinkers and pundits who support the U.S./Israel policy of rejectionism in the Middle East, to those who failed to speak up to expose U.S. aggression in Central America, and to those who act as apologists for the state religion in many other cases. He says that he disagrees with those who think that 'responsible intellectuals' are those who "Speak truth to power," because "the audience is entirely wrong....It is a waste of time and a pointless pursuit to speak truth to Henry Kissinger, or the CEO of General Motors, or others who exercise power in coercive institutions—truths they already know well enough, for the most part" [PP 61]. Rather, the responsible writer addresses those audiences who are in a position to do something about the situations exposed, and rather than speaking to them, they should be speaking with them as a member of a global community concerned with advancing truth and securing social justice for the powerless and the oppressed. But most academics don't do anything of the kind. Establishment intellectuals identify with the interests of the ruling classes and act as their ideological allies in the struggle to keep popular political consciousness within acceptable boundaries. In an essay entitled "Intellectuals and the State" (1977), Chomsky analyzed the emergence of the scientific and technological intelligentsia, as a kind of 'secular priesthood', who work in the service of the established powers of capitalist democracies to exert 'ideological control' over the masses [TNCW 67]. This function is, in his view, necessary to ensure that the masses do not become too politically conscious or aroused.

Those rare intellectuals like, Dewey, and Russell, and of course, Chomsky himself, who depart from this standard form of intellectual dishonesty and attempt to reveal the truth about the system of power—what the Trilateral Commission once described as 'value-oriented intellectuals' who "devote themselves to the derogation of leadership, the challenging of authority, and the unmasking and de-legitimization of established institutions"—often find themselves vilified, ostracized, and labeled as people whose views are 'from Neptune' – that is, as holding views that are outside the bounds of permissible opinion [TNCW 69]. This has been Chomsky's fate in establishment academic, media, and political circles.

Critics of Chomsky's views on the media often point out that his picture is overdrawn and that he fails to mention the extent to which it is possible to gain access to real news and information, if one knows where to look. There is, after all, a vibrant 'alternative press' in America, and magazines and journals such a *The Nation*, *Z Magazine*, and *Mother Jones* regularly publish articles that are critical of U.S. policies and Corporate America. Sometimes these alternative news magazines even publish some of Chomsky's own writings. Similarly there are many independent books and films that tell the stories of, say, the reasons for the Zapatista Rebellion in Chiapas, the class and racial inequalities of American schools, the ongoing struggle for women's equal rights, and many other contemporary social justice issues. Even within the mainstream media, there are occasionally reports and documentaries that are highly critical of American government and its policies: Bob Herbert writes opinions denouncing racism and police brutality for the *New York Times*, Mike Wallace does a story on the failure of SFOR troops to arrest indicted war criminals in Bosnia for CBS, and Christianne Amanpour reports for CNN as American bombs fall on Baghdad. Even Hollywood sometimes tries to tell the truth about corporate influences on news content, as in the film *The Insider*.

But perhaps the most glaring omission from Chomsky's picture of information control is the recent use of the Internet by independent nongovernmental groups campaigning for human rights, debt relief, environmental responsibility, democratic control of corporations, social justice, and a multitude of other progressive issues. For example, after the text of the Multilateral Agreement on Investment (MAI) was leaked and posted on the internet in 1995 an international NGO movement quickly sprang up to oppose it; email messages flashed around the globe decrying its lack of any environmental and human rights provisions, a grassroots campaign was organized, and eventually the treaty had to be withdrawn. Similar global action networks quickly form now around other progressive causes. Aided by the Internet, and global telephone and fax, news about what the G-7, the IMF, World Bank, WTO and other major power players are up to, quickly reaches activists in virtually every country. There are now even web sites, such as The Media Channel, which are devoted to carrying Chomskyan critiques of the mass media. Chomsky provides extensive, detailed documentation of the extent to which reports in the major American media shade the truth, omit crucial facts, and distort current and historical events. However, he rarely acknowledges cases in which the media get it right, and especially, I think, he underrates the new opportunities for meaningful political activism and networking made possible by the Internet. But, it must also be said, that the Internet is rapidly becoming as commercialized as radio and television, and that most of the Web portals that most Web-surfers use just report the same basic corporate content as can be found in the TV networks and glossy magazines. But, as The X-Files viewers know, "The Truth is Out There" – it's just that you have to search for it in some strange places.

Relatively few pages of Chomsky's writings are devoted to describing his positive vision of a just democratic society. Despite his often biting criticisms of contemporary American society, its media, and its corporate-controlled political culture, he remains convinced that, "There are ample opportunities to help create a more humane and decent world, if we choose to act on them" [NI 135]. The system of political control is not all-powerful; "people have the capacity to resist, and sometimes do, with great effect" [NI 134]. For all its faults,

> The United States is a much more civilized place than it was twenty-five years ago. The crisis of democracy and the intellectual independence that so terrified elites have been real enough, and the effects on society have been profound, and on balance generally healthy. The impact is readily discernable over a wide range of concerns, including racism, the environment, feminism, forceful intervention and much else; also in the media, which have allowed some opening to dissident opinion and critical reporting in recent years, considerably beyond what was imaginable even at the peak of the ferment of the sixties, let alone before. [NI 135]

These advances towards greater freedom and social justice have been made mainly "by people who had found ways to escape the system of indoctrination, and the courage and honesty to act," so as to internally constrain the latitude of action of elites, to expose deceit and hypocrisy, and to mitigate state-sponsored violence. Such, "internal constraints within a powerful state provide a margin of survivability for its victims, a fact that should never be forgotten" [NI 134].

Further progress towards the realization of freedom and social justice will require taking "serious steps towards more meaningful democracy [that] would aim to dissolve the concentration of decision-making power, which in our society resides primarily in a state-corporate nexus," and the creation of a "democratic communications policy" that would "seek to develop means of expression and interaction that reflects the interests and concerns of the general population, and encourage their self-education and their individual and collective action" [NI 136]. Chomsky's belief in the capacity for moral wisdom in ordinary people leads him to be optimistic about the prospects for meaningful democratic reforms. As political philosophers Joshua Cohen and Joel Rogers have characterized Chomsky's embrace of this Enlightenment democratic ideal:

Nothing that we know about human nature is inconsistent with the contention that aspirations to freedom and decency are fundamental features of that nature; and nothing that we know about social order defeats the hope that the pursuit of these aspirations will produce significant improvement in human circumstances. The fact that such hopefulness is consistent with the evidence enables children of the Enlightenment to be optimists of the will, without condemning themselves to be irrationalists of the intellect.[63]

Such a humanistic conception of democracy might even merit the much-abused term 'conservative', were it not the case that the meaning of this term has been perverted by contemporary political discourse to mean 'protective of the interests of big business', while the term 'liberal,' which really means 'characterized by liberty,' now means something like 'protective of the interests of big government.' As long as national political debate is conducted in these narrow Orwellian terms, we will miss the point, which is to restore our major social institutions, both government and business, to popular democratic control, by dissolving and dividing the highly concentrated power of the current political, economic, and military elites and devolving effective political and economic power back into the hands of the people. This is the political option we do not hear about on the evening news, which is "hardly a surprise, given its threat to established privilege" [NI 136].

Chomsky is not unaware of the pitfalls and dangers of such a populist course, but his belief in human dignity, in democracy, and in the possibility of moral progress leads him to conclude that such a course presents the best hope for the future of human civilization:

Human beings are the only species with a history. Whether they also have a future is not so obvious. The answer will lie in the prospects for popular movements, with firm roots among all sectors of the population, dedicated to values that are suppressed or driven to the margins within the existing social and political order: community, solidarity, concern for a fragile environment that will have to sustain future generations, creative work under voluntary control, independent thought, and true democratic participation in varied aspects of life. [NI 136]

We humans have at least some creative cognitive capacity to form science and technology, to understand nature and use that understanding for human betterment. We also have the capacity to control illegitimate forms of political, economic and military power, and to remake our governments and economies so that they function to protect human rights and fulfill human needs, while also allowing us to live in harmony with other species and the Earth for countless generations to come. Those who carry on the struggles for freedom, social justice, and ecological sustainability possess the 'ultimate weapon' in grassroots organizing and activism. The dream of a just and free world must not be pushed into the realm of utopias and impossible visions – it can and will become reality if enough people demand it.

But change will only come about through political struggle against the forms of concentrated power that currently block the way forward. There is no historical necessity about continued corporate globalization; it is happening because of the choices we make, and its direction can be altered by our making different, more humane, choices; we being, in particular, the relatively privileged, well educated, and affluent members of global civil society.[64] As beneficiaries of policies carried out in our names that create and perpetuate global inequality, we have a special responsibility to protect the less privileged members of humanity from the injustices done to them in our names. And because of our relative social and technological advantages we also have the opportunity to make a difference that many others, still suffering under the yoke of economic deprivation and political oppression, do not possess. Those of us who now enjoy the freedoms that our forbearers struggled to secure now have the reciprocal moral responsibility to use a portion of our freedom to help others to gain theirs—to pay freedom forward. The more we know about the workings of the current system of unaccountable power, the stronger this responsibility becomes. For those who are willing to accept the responsibility to secure freedom, justice, and dignity for all, -- that is, for all of those philosophers who not only want to interpret the world, but also want to change it – Noam Chomsky's life and work is an inspiration, an education, and a call to action. At the conclusion of our interview I asked him this question:

M.W.: Looking back over your long and distinguished career, what are the things that you are most proud of, the things that you would like to be remembered for? What message would you most like to leave readers of my book about your life and work?

N.C.: That's for other people to answer.

M.W: I thought you'd say that. But I'm interested in what you think.

N.C.: I think about the things I should have done but didn't.

M.W.: OK, I won't press you on it. But you've done a lot and influenced a lot of people.

N.C.: (Smiles).

BIOLIOGRAPHY

WORKS BY NOAM CHOMSKY:

Syntactic Structures. The Hague: Mouton, 1957. [SS]

Current Issues in Linguistic Theory. The Hague: Mouton, 1964. [CILT]

Aspects of the Theory of Syntax. Cambridge, Mass: MIT Press, 1965. [ATS]

Cartesian Linguistics: a Chapter in the History of Rationalist Thought. New York: Harper & Row, 1966. [CL]

Topics in the Theory of Generative Grammar. The Hague: Mouton, 1966. [TTGG]

Language and Mind. New York: Harcourt, Brace Jovanovich, 1968. [LM]

American Power and the New Mandarins. New York: Pantheon, 1969. [APNM]

At War with Asia. New York: Pantheon, 1970. [AWA]

Problems of Knowledge and Freedom: The Russell Lectures. New York: Pantheon, 1971. [PKF]

Studies on the Semantics of Generative Grammar. The Hague: Mouton, 1972. [SSGG]

For Reasons of State. New York: Pantheon, 1973. [FRS]

The Logical Structure of Linguistic Theory. New York: Plenum, 1975. [LSLT]

Reflections on Language. New York: Pantheon, 1975. [RL]

Language and Responsibility. New York: Pantheon, 1979. [LR]

The Washington Connection and Third World Fascism. With Edward S. Herman. Boston, Mass: South End Press, 1979. [WCTWF]

Rules and Representations. New York: Columbia University Press, 1980. [RR]

Towards a New Cold War: Essays on the Current Crisis and How We Got There. New York: Pantheon, 1982. [TNCW]

The Fateful Triangle: The United States, Israel and the Palestinians. Boston, Mass: South End Press, 1983. [FT]

Turning the Tide: U.S. Intervention in Central America and the Struggle for Peace. Boston, Mass: South End Press, 1985. [TT]

On Power and Ideology: The Managua Lectures. Boston, Mass: South End Press, 1987. [PI]

The Culture of Terrorism. Boston, Mass: South End Press, 1988. [CT]

Manufacturing Consent: The Political Economy of the Mass Media. With Edward S. Herman. New York: Pantheon, 1988. [MC]

Necessary Illusions: Thought Control in Democratic Societies. Boston, Mass: South End Press, 1989. [NI]

Deterring Democracy. New York: Verso, 1992. [DD]

Year 501: The Conquest Continues. Boston, Mass: South End Press, 1993. [Y501]

World Orders Old and New. New York: Columbia University Press, 1994. [WOON]

The Minimalist Program. Cambridge, Mass: MIT Press, 1995. [MP]

Power and Prospects: Reflections on Human Nature and the Social Order. Boston, Mass: South End Press, 1996. [PP]

Profit Over People: Neoliberalism and Global Order. New York: Seven Stories Press, 1999. [POP]

The New Military Humanism: Lessons from Kosovo. Monroe, Maine: Common Courage Press, 1999. [NMH]

OTHER WORKS CONSULTED:

Barsky, Robert F. *Noam Chomsky: A Life of Dissent.* Cambridge. Mass: MIT Press, 1998.

Harman, Gilbert Ed. *On Noam Chomsky: Critical Essays.* Garden City NY: Anchor Press, 1974.

Lyons, John. *Noam Chomsky.* New York: Viking Press, 1970.

Maher, John and Judy Groves. *Introducing Chomsky.* New York: Totem Books, 1997.

McGilvray, James. *Chomsky: Language, Mind, and Politics.* Cambridge UK: Polity Press, 1999.

Otero, Carlos. Ed. *Noam Chomsky: Critical Assessments,* 4 volumes. London: Routledge, 1994.

NOTES

[1] The Noam Chomsky Archive. Interview with Marci Randall Miller of KUWR public radio in Laramie, Wyoming. Online http://www.zmag.org/chomsky/index.html. Accessed 11/1/99.

[2] Chomsky has said, "I wish it were possible, as it obviously is not, to deduce from our understanding of human nature that the next stage of social evolution ought to be such and such. That we can't do; at most we can draw very loose tenuous connections that may be more or less suggestive to people." [LP 245]. Quoted in James McGilvray, *Chomsky: Language, Mind, and Politics.* Malden, MA: Polity Press, 1999, p.10.

[3] The senior Dr. Chomsky was a leading Hebrew scholar who served as President of the Faculty of Gratz College for thirty-seven years as well as Professor of Hebrew at Dropsie College, a graduate school of Jewish and Semitic Studies. He was the author of several books, including *How to Teach Hebrew In the Elementary Grades* (1946), and *Hebrew the Eternal Language* (1957).

[4] From an interview with Dr. William Chomsky shortly before his death in 1977. From Carlos Otero. "Chomsky and the Libertarian Tradition: A Renewed Egalitarian Vision, a Coherent Social Theory and Incisive, Up-to-Date Analysis" p. 5 In Carlos P. Otero Ed. *Noam Chomsky: Critical Assessments.* 4 volumes. London: Routledge, 1994. Quoted in David Barsky, *Noam Chomsky: A Life of Dissent.* Cambridge, MA: MIT Press, 1998, p.11.

[5] Interview with James Peck. In James Peck Ed., *The Chomsky Reader.* New York: Pantheon Books, 1987, p. 5.

[6] Barsky, *Noam Chomsky.* Op. cit., p. 15.

[7] Barsky, *Noam Chomsky.* Op. cit., pp. 17-19.

[8] Peck, *The Chomsky Reader.* Op. cit., p. 13.

[9] Barsky, *Noam Chomsky.* Op. cit., pp. 25-26.

[10] Chomsky, APNM, p. 324. Quoted in Barsky, *Noam Chomsky.* Op. cit., p. 35.

[11] LSLT, Introduction, p, 25.

[12] Ibid.

[13] Noam Chomsky, *The Morphophonemics of Modern Hebrew.* New York: Garland, 1979.

[14] For Saussure, *la langue* was "the system of language, the

94

language as a system of forms, whereas *parole* is actual speech, the speech acts made possible by the language. *La langue* is what the individual assimilates when he learns a language, a set of forms "deposited by the practice of speech in speakers who belong to the same community, a grammatical system which, to all intents and purposes, exists in the mind of each speaker"' Quoted in Jonathan Culler, *Ferdinand de Saussure*. New York: Penguin Books, 1976, p. 22.

[15] Zellig Harris, *Structural Linguistics*. Chicago: University of Chicago Press, 1951, p. 1.

[16] Ibid., p.2.

[17] See W. V. O. Quine, *From a Logical Point of View*. Cambridge, Harvard University Press, 1953.

[18] Nelson Goodman, "The Emperor's New Ideas." In Sidney Hook Ed., *Language and Philosophy: A Symposium*. New York: New York University Press, 1969, p. 138.

[19] My approach draws upon recent work in the cognitive philosophy of science dealing with the role that models and analogies have in the process of first formulating scientific theories. See Nancy Nersessian, "How do scientists think? Capturing the dynamics of conceptual change in science," In *Cognitive Models of Science*, R. Giere, Ed., *Minnesota Studies in the Philosophy of Science 15* (Minneapolis: University of Minnesota Press, 1992) pp. 3-45.

[20] Noam Chomsky and Jerrold Katz, "What the linguist is talking about." *Journal of Philosophy*. 71 (1974): 347-67, p. 349.

[21] See Noam Chomsky, "Explanatory Models in Linguistics." In E. Nagel, P. Suppes, and A Tarski (Eds.), *Logic. Methodology and the Philosophy of Science: Proceedings of the 1960 International Congress of the Philosphy of Science Association*. Palo Alto CA: Stanford University Press, 1962, pp. 528-550; Noam Chomsky. *Syntactic Structures*. The Hague: Mouton, 1957; and N. Chomsky. "A Review of B.F. Skinner's *Verbal Behavior*." *Language* 35, no. 1 (1959), pp. 26-58.

[22] See. W.V.O. Quine, "Two Dogmas of Empiricism." In W. V. O. Quine. *From a Logical Point of View*. Cambridge, Mass: Harvard University Press, 1953, pp. 20-46.

[23] Cf. Nelson Goodman, "The New Riddle of Induction." In N. Goodman. *Fact, Fiction, and Forecast*. New York: Bobbs-Merrill, 1955. pp. 59-83.

[24] Noam Chomsky, "Review of B.F. Skinner's *Verbal Behavior*" Reprinted in Jerry A. Fodor and Jerrold J. Katz Eds., *The Structure of Language: Readings in the Philosophy of Language*. Englewood Cliffs NJ: Prentice-Hall, 1964. , p. 574.

[25] Chomsky dislikes the term 'innateness hypothesis' and rarely uses it. I employ it only because it is commonly used to refer to this aspect of his thought.

[26] In many of Chomsky's later writings, he drops the analogy in which language learning is portrayed as a process akin to theory construction in favor of a more biological conception which likens language acquisition to the growth of bodily organs. This shift notwithstanding, the textual evidence from his early writing provides ample evidence that he *arrived* at his "innateness hypothesis' by means of the analogy with theory construction, even though he later abandoned that way of presenting it.

[27] See Gilbert Harman (Ed.), *On Noam Chomsky: Critical Essays*. Garden City: Anchor Books, 1974.

[28] Speaking of the "Cognitive Revolution" Chomsky says, "it wasn't all that much of a revolution in my opinion." [PP 1].

[29] Barsky, *Noam Chomsky*. Op. cit., p. 107.

[30] See for example his remarks in Chapter 1 of MP.

[31] Noam Chomsky. "The Current Scene in Linguistics." College English 27 (1966), p. 591.

[32] See Jerry A. Fodor, *The Modularity of Mind*, Cambridge, MA: MIT Press, 1983 for the more or less canonical discussion of this approach to cognitive science.

[33] Chomsky is referring to the work of Prince Peter Alekseyevich Kropotkin, in particular his *Mutual Aid: A Factor of Evolution*. 2nd Edition. London: Heineman, 1904.

[34] Readers interested in exploring these technical details should consult McGilvray's *Chomsky: Language, Mind, and Politics* op. cit., N. Chomsky and H. Lasnik. "The theory of principles and parameters." In J. Jacobs, A. von Stechow, W. Sternefield, and T. Venneman, eds. *Syntax: An International Handbook of Contemporary Research* . Berlin: de Gruyer, 1993; or Chomsky's *The Minimalist Program*, which although it represents a later stage in the development of this approach, does provide a good discussion of the specific developments that led up to it.

[35] Quoted in McGilvray, Op. cit. p. 148.

[36] David Barsky, *Noam Chomsky*. Op. cit. p.103.

[37] Chomsky has discussed his decision to plunge into the Anti-war movement in his interview with James Peck. See *The Chomsky Reader.* Op. cit. "Interview," esp. pp. 54-55.

[38] Chomsky was the commencement speaker at my graduation from Swarthmore College in May of 1970, shortly after the U.S. began bombing Cambodia and several days after a childhood friend of mine, Allison Krause, had been shot dead at Kent State University by the Ohio National Guard. I don't recall exactly what he said, but do remember that his speech made a big impression on me and my fellow student anti-war activists at the time.

[39] Chomsky does not believe that sovereignty is an end in itself. In a recent lecture he wrote: "Sovereignty is no value in itself. It's only a value insofar as it relates to freedom and rights, either enhancing them or diminishing them. I want to take for granted something that may seem obvious, but is actually controversial--namely that, in speaking of freedom and rights, we have in mind human beings; that is, persons of flesh and blood, not abstract political and legal constructions like corporations, or states, or capital." From "Control of Our Lives" Kiva Auditorium, Albuquerque, New Mexico, February 26, 2000. Online ZNET Chomsky Archive. Accessed 05/11/00.

[40] James McGilvray has observed that in his political writings, but not in his scientific works, Chomsky "makes extensive use of the rhetorical device of irony....Irony requires that a person have the cognitive machinery needed to recognize that what is said is not the correct story. Irony presupposes, then, not just that a person has the concepts involved but that he or she can apply them, comprehending enough of what is going on to recognize that what is being said is false, misleading, or perhaps evasive." McGilvary, *Chomsky.* Op. cit. p. 19.

[41] He means the Universal Declaration of Human Rights (1948), which is the foundation document of the contemporary human rights movement and is regarded as customary international law. Chomsky has expounded on his thoughts on the hypocritical U.S. stance toward human rights see his "Letter from Lexington" in Lies of Our Times, June 18, 1993. ZNET Chomsky Archives.

[42] Noam Chomsky, "Answering Some Queries about Moral Principles and International Law." ZNET Daily Commentaries, May 9, 1999. Online: http://zena.secureform.com/zdaily/. Accessed 05/08/00.

[43] This is another one of Chomsky's ironies; he is alluding to the famous "Four Freedoms" Speech by Franklin Delano Roosevelt in

January 1941 in which the president urged that the war in Europe was being waged to safeguard 'four freedoms': freedom of speech, freedom of worship, freedom from fear, and freedom from want.

[44] For documentation see Nick Cullather, *Secret History: The CIA's Classified Account of Its Operations in Guatemala, 1952-1954*. Palo Alto: Stanford University Press, 2000. Also, highly recommended for its analysis of the development of U.S. counterinsurgency doctrine is Michael McClintock, *Instruments of Statecraft: U.S. Guerrilla Warfare, Counterinsurgency, Counterterrorism 1940-1990*. New York:Pantheon, 1992.

[45] Chomsky cites the testimony of former CIA agent Ralph McGehee who was, before his defection, privy to the (still) secret CIA history of the 1965 Indonesian operation. [CR 305]. Chomsky provided extensive documentation of these and subsequent events in *The Washington Connection and Third World Fascism: The Political Economy of Human Rights* Volume 1 (with Edward Herman). Boston: South End Press, 1979.

[46] For Chomsky's views on the role of the Indonesian military in the atrocities of 1999, see his remarks in "East Timor Retrospective" ZNET Chomsky Archives. Accessed 4/12/00. For corroboration of the role of the Indonesian military see the report of the UN Commission of Inquiry into these events published in January 2000.

[47] For the whole grim and depressing history of these events see Henry Kamm, *Cambodia: Report from a Stricken Land*. New York: Arcade Publishing, 1998.

[48] Chomsky's most extended discussion of these issues is in *The Fateful Triangle: The United States, Israel and the Palestinians*, Boston: South End, 1983. But there have been numerous subsequent discussions as events have unfolded.

[49] The Israeli Army withdrew from Southern Lebanon in June 2000.

[50] "The Israel-Arafat Agreement" *Z Magazine*, October 1993. Chomsky Archives on ZNET.

[51] "Israel, Lebanon, and the 'Peace Process'" April 23, 1996. Chomsky Archives on ZNET.

[52] Ibid.

[53] On February 7, 2000, Human Rights Watch claimed that, "About five hundred civilians died in ninety separate incidents as a result of NATO bombing in Yugoslavia." According to Kenneth

Roth, HRW's Executive Director, "Once it made the decision to attack Yugoslavia, NATO should have done more to protect civilians."

[54] See "Amnesty International Calls for a Halt to Helicopter Transfers" AI Index EUR 44/06/96 (http://www.amnesty.org/news/1996/44400696.htm accessed 11/2/99).

[55] On the idea of 'moral competence' see: Susan Dywer, "Moral Competence." In *Philosophy and Linguistics*. Kumiko Murasuji Ed. Boulder CO: Westview Press, 1999.

[56] Michael Walzer, *Thick and Thin: Moral Argument at Home and Abroad*. Notre Dame, IN: University of Notre Dame Press, 1994, pp. 57-58.

[57] Chomsky's interpretation of U.S. history is very close that advanced by Charles Beard in his *An Economic Interpretation of the Constitution*. See also, Howard Zinn. *A People's History of the United States*. New York: HarperCollins, 1995 (esp. pp. 89-101).

[58] Morton Horwitz, *The Transformation of American Law*. Quoted in Howard Zinn. *A People's History of the United States*. Op. cit., p. 235.

[59] Zinn, Op .cit. p. 255.

[60] See Robert W. McChesney, "The New Global Media." *The Nation* November 29, 1999.

[61] Noam Chomsky, "Taking Control of Our Lives" op. cit.

[62] For one such eyewitness account, see Paul Hawkin, "N30: Journal of the Uninvited." *Whole Earth Magazine*. 100 (Spring 2000): 28-37.

[63] Quoted by V. K. Ramachandran in "An Unjust War" Frontline Interview, March 2-15, 1991. Online ZNET Chomsky Archives. Accessed 05/11/00.

[64] Chomsky refers to the view that corporate-led globalization is somehow inevitable as "TINA" (There Is No Alternative). He characterizes TINA as "a farcical mimicry of vulgar Marxism" and as a "self-serving fraud."

ABOUT THE AUTHOR

Morton Winston was born in Philadelphia and raised in Pittsburgh, Pennsylvania. He attended Swarthmore College graduating with High Honors and Phi Beta Kappa with a double major in philosophy and psychology. He also attended the University of Illinois at Urbana-Champaign, completing an M.A. in psycholinguistics, and a Ph.D. in philosophy of science. Dr. Winston has been affiliated with the Department of Philosophy and Religion at the College of New Jersey since 1979, where he is currently Professor of Philosophy. His previous books include: *Explanation in Linguistics: A Critique of Generative Grammar*, *The Philosophy of Human Rights*, and *Society, Ethics, and Technology*. Dr. Winston has also pursued a parallel career as a human rights activist with Amnesty International. From 1985-1991 he served as Director of the South Africa Coordination Group of Amnesty International USA. He served on AIUSA's national Board of Directors from 1991 to 1997, and was Chair of the Board. He is currently Chair of the Standing Committee on Organization and Development of Amnesty International.